OW
HOLY WRIT
WAS
WRITTEN

c44/8

HOW HOLY WRIT WAS WRITTEN

O.C. EDWARDS, JR.

Abingdon Press
Nashville

How Holy Writ Was Written

Copyright © 1989 by Abingdon Press

All rights reserved.

This book is printed on acid-free paper.

Edwards, O. C. (Otis Carl), 1928-
   How Holy Writ was written: the story of the New Testament/O. C. Edwards, Jr.
      p. cm.
   ISBN 0-687-17768-5 (alk. paper)
      1. Bible. N.T.—Introductions. I. Title.
   BS2330.2.E3 1989   89-32016
   225.6'6—dc20   CIP

MANUFACTURED BY THE PARTHENON PRESS AT
NASHVILLE, TENNESSEE, UNITED STATES OF AMERICA

To
my teacher and friend,
Robert M. Grant

ὁ θαυμασιώτατος Ἰουστῖνος

CONTENTS

PREFACE

The purpose of this book is to provide people interested in the New Testament with the latest insights of scholars into how and why its books were written. An attempt is made to communicate the results of recent research in language that does not presuppose technical training. This effort is made out of the conviction that the understanding scholars have of such topics will not only be interesting to ordinary Bible readers but that it will also deepen their insight into what the sacred writers were trying to say and thus assist the readers in making progress in their Christian living. This book does not provide all the information normally included in the sort of volume called an "introduction," but is limited instead to issues connected with the writing process. To the extent that it fits exactly into any of the sub-disciplines of New Testament study, it attempts to share the findings of redaction criticism.

This book can serve as a textbook for a group—such as an adult church school class—or it can be read by an individual who wishes to pursue the subject. The questions at the end of each chapter, therefore, could assist in either class discussion or private reflection. They are not designed to discover how accurately readers have remembered the information so much as to assist them in deciding what to make of it; they focus not on the data but on the significance of the data. Thus there are no "correct" answers. As they say in courtrooms, a conclusion is called for on the part of the witness. The intention is that readers will be enabled to continue their faith journeys with deeper understanding.

Very few, if any, of the findings reported here represent discoveries of my own. The task is the humbler one of communicating what others have found out. This realization causes me to be very aware of the teachers from whom I learned what I now try to pass on to others. It is appropriate, therefore, that the book be dedicated to the scholar who directed my doctoral research and who has guided me in so many other ways. At the same time I wish to express gratitude to my other teachers. It was my parents who first taught me to love the Bible as they also taught so many members of their Methodist church school classes. The one disappointment of this undertaking is that my mother died while the project was under way and thus will not have the fun of teaching from a text that her son wrote.

More formally, though, I wish to acknowledge my debt to my academic instructors: Dean R. E. Smith of Centenary College; E. F. Scott, Kenneth Clark, Franklin Young, and W. D. Davies at Duke Divinity School; Pierson Parker at the General Theological Seminary; and the dedicatee, Robert Grant of the University of Chicago. And, although Norman Perrin arrived at Chicago after I had gone out of residence, I must acknowledge my great debt for his informal tutelage. Since leaving school, I have learned much from colleagues, especially Richard Pervo here at Seabury-Western. And I have been greatly stimulated by teaching with Robert Jewett and Richard Stegner, colleagues across the street at Garrett-Evangelical.

C H A P T E R

O N E

The Book
That Is a Library

Raising the Question

According to the old proverb, "Familiarity breeds contempt." It may not always breed contempt, but it does often leave us with a sense that we understand whoever or whatever is familiar. A case in point is an acquaintance of mine who found video cassette recorders mystifying. When I acknowledged that I did not even understand television, my friend had to make the same admission. The VCR was recognized as strange because it was also relatively new; the television was assumed to be in the realm of the known because it was in the realm of the frequently encountered.

The same principle applies to people. We assume that the behavior of people we see often is predictable, but we must admit that it surprises us regularly. What's more, the better we know people, the more often they surprise us. Most married people will admit under pressure that they really don't understand their spouses at all. Certainly, the people we know best are the hardest for us to describe to someone else; we know so many exceptions to every generalization that it is difficult to leave any unqualified.

The Bible affects many of us in the same way. Nothing could be more familiar to Christians, but even the greatest scholars will admit that there is much about it that they don't know. And many of the things we take for granted prove not to be the case. For instance, we have a barely resistible tendency to think of the Bible as one book. After all, it comes bound together as a single volume. Whether it is a large pulpit edition* or is a small personal Bible, whether it is something beautiful bound in leather and printed on thin sheets of India paper with gold edges or is sturdily bound in buckram with footnotes for study or is paperbacked and economically printed, it's all bound together as one book.

Yet, it is more complicated than that. Even though people sometimes say, "The Bible says," they know that things are not said by the Bible as a whole but appear in individual parts of it. No matter how little people know about the Bible, they know at least that it is divided into two main sections. Indeed, the New Testament is often printed alone, although the Hebrew Scriptures (commonly called the Old Testament) are seldom published that way. And everyone knows that the divisions of both of these sections are called "books."

Still we are in the habit of thinking of the Bible as a single inspired volume of writings that is authoritative for our religion. And so it is. But precisely because of its importance we need to understand it as well as we can. This understanding involves an awareness that rather than being a single book, the Bible is a whole library of books that bring together material created over a time span of more than two thousand years in places as far apart as modern Iran and Italy. This library consists of thirty-nine books of the Hebrew Scriptures together with the twenty-seven of

---

*Pulpit and lectern Bibles are the same thing; the difference is in the piece of church furniture they are placed on in different churches.

the New Testament; nowadays it often has bound with it the eighteen books that are called the Apocrypha.

When confronted with the idea of so many books produced over so many centuries in such widely differing places and cultures, one does not have to be much of a romantic to begin to wonder how these books came into existence. Just a little thought on that question can produce a perspective that is often overlooked. *These books were all written by people!* So accustomed are we to thinking of these works as authoritative and inspired that it is easy to be under the impression that they just appeared, handed down from heaven already written or as stenographic recordings of oracular words or, at the very least, as the automatic writing of persons in trancelike states. But the God Christians worship does not override human agency; instead, this God accomplishes most of the divine purposes through human beings. When God decided upon a full self-revelation, the form was full human existence as Jesus the Christ. It is hardly likely, then, that the authoritative writings of Christians would bypass the involvement of men and women and suddenly appear, like the modern sanitary products that boast that they are "untouched by human hands."

Instead, God's inspiration of the Bible was accomplished through animating individual communities and persons to understand their own unique experience and situation from the perspective of God and to make that understanding known through writing. It should be noted here that communities, as well as single individuals, are regarded as the producers of biblical books. That may sound strange to contemporary ears, since our culture has come to think of authorship so completely as the activity of an isolated person, but during the long period that the scriptures were being written, the notion of the individual had not fully emerged in human consciousness. Certainly, our ideas of the author as an artist engaged in aesthetic creativity did not arise until recent times.

However, individual or group, particular people at particular times and places wrote all the documents that make up our Bible for reasons that made sense to them in terms of the practical situations of their religious communities. Once that fact becomes clear to us, it will be followed immediately by the insight that our understanding of these writings would be greatly increased if we knew who wrote them and why. Another way of saying that is that our insight into what a biblical passage *means* for us today will be deepened by finding out what it *meant* to the people to whom it was originally addressed.

In so short a book it would be impossible to do justice to the circumstances under which all the books of the Bible and Apocrypha were written, so attention will be confined to the twenty-seven books of the New Testament. But even that is quite a library by itself. Because we value these books as sacred writings, we want to know everything we can about them. How *did* this Holy Writ come to be written? The rest of this book will be devoted to answering that question.

The Bible Before the New Testament

A necessary prelude to learning how New Testament books were written is learning what concept of sacred writings existed before the New Testament books came into being and what documents were included in that category—that is, what concept of a "Bible" existed and what writings made it up. Crucial to understanding that is noting the distinction between the process by which the books were *written* and the process by which they were *recognized* to be authoritative for the religious community.

The earliest material in the Hebrew Scriptures originated in oral form almost two thousand years before the time of

Christ. It and other traditions were included in a written collection that appeared about a thousand years later. But it was not until five hundred years after that, sometime after 500 B.C., that this written collection, much added to and edited, came to be regarded as holy. This collection, consisting of the first five books of the Bible, is called the Pentateuch by modern scholars, but the people of Israel referred to it as *Torah*, a Hebrew word that is often translated as "law," but that is better rendered "teaching" or "instruction." The eighth and ninth chapters of Nehemiah, which tell of how Ezra read the "book of the law of Moses" to the people of Israel after their return from exile in Babylon, seem to be an account of how these books became the religious constitution of Israel and the terms of its agreement with God.

The second collection of writings that came to be regarded as holy in Israel was known by the Hebrew word for *Prophets*, although it includes more than the written works of the great prophets from the centuries before and after the Babylonian exile in the sixth century B.C. Also included are books that today are considered historical (Joshua through II Kings, with the exception of Ruth). These historical writings were known as "the former prophets," while the works of the writing prophets were called "the latter prophets." The works of the latter prophets had some degree of inspiration attributed to them from the beginning, since those who spoke these oracles often claimed that they were "the Word of the Lord." Yet, all that is certain about when they came to be regarded as somewhat on a par with the Torah is that the process seems to have been completed before the time of Jesus.

The remaining books of the Hebrew Scriptures are called the *Writings*. The first reference to a list of authoritative books that includes any of these Writings is in the preface to the Apocryphal book of Ecclesiasticus, or Sirach. The author of this preface is the person who translated the book from Hebrew into Greek. He says that it was written by his grandfather, who had devoted himself to "the reading of the law and the prophets and *the other books of our fathers.*" That preface can be dated to around 132 B.C. The next reference to all three sections of the Hebrew Scriptures is in Luke's story of Jesus' resurrection appearance to his followers; there Jesus says he had told them that everything spoken about him "in the law of Moses and the prophets and the psalms" had to be fulfilled (24:44).

An authoritative list of biblical books, such as that implied by these three categories of books, is called a *canon*—a word related to the English word *cane*, a material from which ancient equivalents of yardsticks were made. Thus the word means a standard. Even though the Torah, the Prophets, and some of the Writings were regarded as authoritative before the time of Jesus, there appears to have been no definitive list until near the end of the first century A.D. By then two things had happened: first the Jews had failed in a tragic effort to eject their Roman conquerors and, second, Christianity had begun to offer serious competition to Judaism throughout the Greco-Roman world.

Since the Babylonian exile (sixth century B.C.) Jews had been dispersed throughout the civilized world of the time and had become very strong in a number of places (see Acts 2:9-11), including such centers of Greek culture as Alexandria, Egypt. To meet the needs and reflect the faith of such people, a considerable body of Jewish religious writing began to appear in Greek, either as translations from Hebrew originals (such as Sirach) or as original compositions (like much of the rest of the Apocrypha). When competition between the young Christian church and the synagogue began, some of these Greek writings were very useful in defending the Christian church's position as the true Israel. But was this collection of Greek writings a part of "the Writings"? Were they authoritative?

After the Jewish-Roman war, a group of Jewish scholars settled in Jamnia (or Jabneh), a town on the Palestinian coast, and began to rebuild their religious community as well as they could after the destruction of Jerusalem and its Temple. In order to get things on a firm footing again, they had to define many things that had been undefined before. One of these was to make the first list of authoritative books. This move was necessary in the transition from being a religion of cultic sacrifice to being a religion of a book that was under way in Judaism. Not surprisingly, the Greek books that could be used to Christian advantage were excluded. The list the Jabneh scholars came up with is that of the Old Testament books that appear in most Protestant editions of the Bible.

The Jabneh decisions, however, appear to have been binding mainly on areas where Semitic languages were still strong. There were other areas in which Greek was the main or only language of the Jews. Since the third century B.C., they had begun to translate their holy books into Greek, and they even had legends that the translation had been performed identically by seventy(-two) scholars under divine inspiration. Thus the translation is called the Septuagint, from the Latin word for seventy, and is referred to as the Roman numeral LXX by scholars. Those Jews of the Dispersion who used the Septuagint do not seem to have felt bound by the decision of the scholars at Jamnia, since they continued to use a longer canon that included the books of the Apocrypha.

Historically, the LXX that included the Apocrypha became the first Bible of the early Christians, their Bible before there was a New Testament. The religion of Jesus had attracted relatively few adherents in his homeland, and it was not until it began to move into the Greco-Roman world in the middle of the first century A.D. that it began to make many converts. These were the Greek-speaking

Christians who used the Septuagint. Its list of books was authoritative among most Christians until the Reformation of the sixteenth century, when some Christians wanted to accept the canon of Jabneh as their own. Their decision to do so accounts for the appearance of Protestant Bibles without the Apocrypha. The Eastern Orthodox and Roman Catholic churches, however, have always used Bibles in which the books Protestants call apocryphal were integrated into the Old Testament.

The Holiness of the Writ

A good bit has been said about the canon as a list of authoritative books, but so far nothing has been said about what the books are authoritative for. One of the first things that can be noted is that the books listed can be read at public worship. The King James Version of the Bible is also known as the Authorized version. It is authorized to be read at the services of the Church of England.

This use of Scripture does not appear to go back as far as once was believed. For a long time it was assumed that synagogues originated during the Babylonian exile (sixth century B.C.). More recently, scholars have begun to wonder why, if synagogues existed so early, references to them in literature and archaeological remains of them are all so late. The evidence for their existence around the time of Christ is strong. It seems likely that they must have been developing in the previous century or two. Luke's account of Jesus' sermon in the synagogue at Nazareth gives one of the earliest descriptions of what the services were like (4:16-30). From Luke and other sources a picture is derived of lessons read from the Torah and the Prophets, followed by comment on the readings and prayers, although some scholars doubt that a regular cycle of readings existed so early.

At any rate, one of the things that inclusion in the canon

meant was that the writing could be used at worship. A later expression referred to canonical writings as scrolls that "defile the hands." This is to say that they were holy and that rules of ceremonial purity must be observed in connection with them. This attitude is close to that of Christian churches in the liturgical tradition that have special ceremonies in relation to Bible reading, such as a procession in which the book of the Gospels is taken to where it can be read in the midst of the congregation. The deacon carrying the book can be preceded by a cross and candles and possibly incense. The same spirit of reverence for the sacred book is seen in evangelical homes in which it is thought inappropriate to place anything on top of the Bible.

In addition to its being read in worship, the canonical status of a biblical book is connected with such concepts as "the Word of God," "revelation," and "inspiration." All of these indicate that the writings so described are reliable guides to Christian belief and practice. This attitude is summarized in II Timothy 3:16: "All scripture is inspired by God and profitable for teaching, for reproof, for correction and for training in righteousness." However, the Scriptures referred to here were still the Septuagint.

Interesting early examples of the doctrinal interpretation of biblical books may be found in the Dead Sea Scrolls, especially in the Habakkuk Commentary. The sectarians who wrote the Scrolls saw Habakkuk as having predicted the events that led to the foundation of their community. The New Testament employs a similar kind of interpretation, but it sees the numerous passages cited from the Hebrew Scriptures as being veiled predictions of the coming of Christ. Galatians 4:21-31 is an example of this; in it Paul interprets what Genesis has to say about the two sons of Abraham as referring to the relation of the young church to Israel.

Part of what was thought to be involved in the doctrinal

authority of books of Scripture was an assumption that what they said was true in almost any sense in which it could be taken. Or, possibly, the idea was that the Holy Spirit had not made all biblical revelation explicit but had hidden passages among the sacred pages that had to be decoded in order to be understood. The passage from Galatians referred to above is a case in point. Nothing in the Genesis text says that Ishmael refers to Israel and Isaac to the church; Paul only assumes that the passage has that meaning. This kind of interpretation, which thinks that everything in biblical passages refers to something else and has to be decoded term by term, is called *allegorical interpretation.* The technique was borrowed from Greek philosophers, who used it on the works of Homer. It was the major form of biblical interpretation used by the Christian church until well after the Reformation. It is an extreme example of the extent to which Christians have regarded the Bible as authoritative for doctrine. While the Bible remains the chief authority for the belief of most Christian bodies today, many no longer see that authority in anything but the literal meaning of the Bible.

The other area in which the authority of the canon is to be seen is behavior. This includes not only ethics and morals but religious observances as well. The Pharisees who were contemporaries of Jesus, for instance, believed that the kingdom of God would come if all Israel would observe for just one day the rules for ceremonial purity that the Hebrew Scriptures prescribe for priests when they are actually officiating in the Temple. And all down the centuries Christians have sought standards for their own moral practice in the Ten Commandments, the Sermon on the Mount, various passages from the letters of Paul, and other parts of the Bible.

Three things, therefore, appear to be involved in any minimal understanding of canonical authority: the writings within the canon may be (1) read in worship; (2) consulted for doctrine; and (3) relied upon for norms of behavior. These qualities were already attributed to the Hebrew Scriptures at the time the New Testament was being written. Understanding that is important background for seeing how the New Testament, the library of books to be considered in this book, came into being.

THINGS TO THINK ABOUT

1. What difference does it make to think of the Bible as a library of books as well as a single book?
2. Does it make you look at biblical books in a new way to think of them as written by individual people? By communities?
3. Why did the recognition of books as inspired come so long after they were written?
4. What is involved for you in the concept of biblical inspiration?

CHAPTER

TWO

The Spoken Word

As we have said, this book is concerned with how certain writings came to be written. A necessary preliminary to that writing process, however, was a time when words were not written but spoken. In fact, one could speak of three periods during that oral stage: (1) the time during the ministry of Jesus, when he was addressing his opponents, sympathizers, and assistants; (2) the time when information about Jesus was being passed on by word of mouth; and (3) the time when the sayings of Jesus were being formed into the collection scholars call Q. This chapter will deal with those three periods.

Redemption in a Time of Reform

The story of the creation of the New Testament is a part of the story of the rise of Christianity, and it is hard to understand that part without some idea of the whole. There is no room here for a full account of the emergence of the church or even for a summary of what is recorded about it in the New Testament. Instead, an effort will be made to see the movement Jesus started against its background in the other religious movements in Palestine during his lifetime.

Anyone old enough to remember the Great Depression in the United States has a fair idea of what social and economic conditions were like in Palestine at the time of Jesus. The Depression was a time when many people became homeless and wandered in search of work. In addition to the sort of migration to California, described in Steinbeck's *Grapes of Wrath*, many transients—called by such names as hobos or tramps—begged from door to door and traveled the country on freight trains. Not surprisingly, many (in absolute numbers if not proportionally) of the unemployed turned to crime. Besides the bootleggers and others who cashed in on the opportunities afforded by Prohibition, there were bank robbers and desperadoes like John Dillinger, "Pretty Boy" Floyd, and Clyde Barrow and Bonnie Parker. Many troubled people who turned to religion for comfort and help were taken advantage of in one way or another by religious sensationalists like Aimee Semple McPherson, Father Coughlin, and Father Divine. One of the pioneers in the sociological interpretation of the New Testament, Gerd Theissen, has seen the same sort of figures in the Palestine of Jesus' day: "Anyone dissatisfied with things as they were could become a criminal or a healer, a beggar or a prophet, a man possessed or an exorcist" (*The Sociology of Early Palestinian Christianity*, p. 36).

Times were hard. Palestine was about the size of New Hampshire, and much of the land was not suitable for agriculture. The population of the country was about 2.5 million, more than could be supported by the arable land. Most of the usual expedients for dealing with overpopulation—such as military conquest or colonization—were not options. A tiny wealthy class of Roman landlords and Jewish aristocracy collaborated with the Romans, and the rest of the population was divided between a small middle class of artisans and merchants and a large group of peasants who either owned modest family farms or worked as day laborers. As this implies, the majority of the population was rural rather than urban.

The biggest trouble of all was that the nation was occupied by a foreign power. For almost six hundred years the nation that regarded itself as God's chosen people had endured the galling embarrassment of being a possession of whatever empire ruled the Middle East at the time. For about a century that empire had been Roman. While Roman occupation touched the lives of ordinary people in rural areas in few ways, there was at least one in which its impact was devastating: taxation. Roman political taxation, in addition to the full system of religious taxation imposed by the Temple, meant that the average peasant farm had a tax burden of about 40 percent of its produce—too much for what remained to support a family of subsistence farmers.

Amid such ferment, a plethora of individuals and groups offered solutions. As the Gospels indicate, some of the dispossessed became bandits. These, on the whole, seem to have confined their attentions to people with enough money to steal, and they maintained good relations with the poor. Often, in fact, they were perceived as defenders of the helpless and were regarded as Robin Hoods. During the time of Jesus, these groups do not appear to have been guerrillas trying to drive out the Roman conquerors, but such groups did form in time for the revolt of A.D. 66–70.

Not surprisingly, many of the protest movements took on a religious character. Jewish thought at the time saw the situation as so grave that human action could not retrieve it. Heavenly intervention must occur on behalf of God's people. Thus prophets appeared, promising or announcing that intervention either by pronouncing oracles, as the classic prophets had done, or by forming liberation movements, as Moses had done, to make their prophecies self-fulfilling. Other movements also arose in which particular figures announced themselves to be the one ordained by God for the release of the people.

In addition to these movements under "bandits, prophets, and messiahs," as a recent book title calls them, there were also reform movements within Judaism that had the status of religious parties. The *Sadducees*, familiar from the Gospels, are one party of the time, but they were not in favor of reform. They were members of the wealthy priestly aristocracy and had a large investment in maintaining the status quo. The *Pharisees*, though, as noted above, wanted to see Israel obey in daily life all the rules for ceremonial purity required of a priest functioning in the Temple; they expected such obedience by "a nation of priests" to inaugurate God's reign on earth. Thus they devoted careful attention to interpreting all the regulations of the Torah in such a way that they could be certain none would be disobeyed by accident. Another reform movement was the *Essenes*, the group believed to have produced the Dead Sea Scrolls. They had originated over a century and a half before, when one of the brothers of Judas Maccabeus had claimed to be king and high priest. They thought that a king must be a descendent of David and a high priest a descendent of Solomon's high priest Zadok. Thus they withdrew from worship in the Temple and formed their community on the bank of the Dead Sea. A fourth party, the *Zealots*, is sometimes described as a reform movement, but, as noted above, such guerrilla movements appear to have been organized after the time of Jesus, much nearer the beginning of the revolt against Rome.

Many birds and animals are able to defend themselves because their coloring allows them to fit in with their background so well that they are hard to see. Although Christians looking back two thousand years to the time of their Lord inevitably recognize his uniqueness and consider it appropriate that time be dated before and after him, this review of the context of his ministry suggests that to contemporary viewers he must have been as well camouflaged as these birds and animals. That fact should disturb no one's faith, since the Gospels, Mark especially, suggest that even Jesus' closest followers did not really understand him until after the resurrection.

Jesus left his hometown and spent his ministry as a traveling prophet in the rural region around the Lake of Galilee. While he appears to have made Capernaum his headquarters in some way, the impression one gets is of someone on the road. That meant that he was dependent on the financial support of others. Yet the Gospels do not give an impression of closely defined communities of people who accepted his message in the towns and villages to which he went. His network of support seems very loose.

Yet the support required was not for him alone. The Gospels talk about a group of at least twelve who traveled with him as his staff, a group that represented the symbolic reestablishment of the twelve tribes of Israel. These staff members had sacrificed their means of livelihood, the security of living at home, and the regular company of their families to accompany Jesus. They must have led a very vulnerable existence. There also appears to have been a looser group of followers who accompanied Jesus and the Twelve. These are the people referred to as "disciples" in passages where that term is not limited to the Twelve. It is not clear whether this group had a more or less constant membership or instead consisted of persons who came and went. The Gospels give no clear idea of how large this group was, nor is the length of this itinerate ministry known.

The message that Jesus preached as he went from town to town was that the rule, reign, and kingdom of God was about to break into history through his proclamation of it. The underlying assumption is a world view that scholars call "apocalyptic," which has a root meaning of "revelatory." This world view considers history to be under the control of the forces of evil, Satan and his army of unclean spirits or demons. Their control over history is being broken and God's control is being reestablished through Jesus' proclamation of this good news. That it is through Jesus' preaching that God's control over history is being restored implies a very high status for Jesus himself, but Jesus says little about his own role. His message concerns the reign of God and not himself.

Jesus' message is very different from that of the other reform movements of his time. For instance, what he required of those who recognized the inbreaking of the reign of God and accepted its authority over their lives was not so much the religious behavior sought by the Pharisees or the community of the Dead Sea Scrolls. Rather, it had mainly to do with how people treated one another. By the same token, he did not preach hatred or participate in or dream about military action against enemies, as the Essenes, bandits, and, later, the Zealots did. Earthly rule did not seem to interest him. His program seemed to be one of peace, of reconciliation between God and human beings, and of reconciliation of human beings with one another. Thus the Jesus movement as a reform movement almost disappears against the background of its time; the major difference between it and other reform movements seems to be in the program for reform that it offers. It is only by the hindsight of faith that one can look back and say that in this ministry may be seen God's definitive effort for the reclamation of a lost world.

Between the Events and the Written Record

It is easy to presume that what happened to the followers of Jesus after the ascension is well known because it is recorded in the book of Acts. Just a little thought, however, can show that this presumption is untrue even if one does not bring into question the accuracy of Acts. For instance, the latter half of Acts is devoted to the missionary career of Paul, but nowhere does it mention that Paul wrote letters to his congregations, letters that make up a sizable portion of the New Testament. So not everything modern Christians would want to know about the years after the departure of Jesus is contained in Acts.

One of the things that Acts does not tell is how the memory of Jesus was preserved before the Gospels were written down. About all that Acts suggests can be seen in its speeches, most of which have a similar outline. The speeches begin with pointing out that something was prophesied in the Hebrew Scriptures; next they point out that this prophecy was fulfilled by Jesus and that the apostles were witnesses of that fact. The hearers, therefore, are called upon to repent and believe the gospel.

It does seem likely that the early church spent much time reading the Hebrew Scriptures in search for passages that could be understood as prophecies about Jesus. A good bit of New Testament theology consists of arguments that certain passages of Hebrew Scriptures predicted things that Jesus did.

Of nothing is this so true as the death of Jesus. One can read the story of Jesus' arrest, trial, and execution in Mark, for instance, and see the whole sequence of events as having been foretold in Psalms 22 and 69 and in the fifty-third chapter of Isaiah. While some scholars believe that Mark himself is responsible for the writing of the record of Holy Week that he passes on, it seems unlikely that he was the first to raise these issues and to come to conclusions about them. No question could have been so important to the first Christians as showing how the One they claimed to be God's agent of salvation could have died a death that Deuteronomy 21:23 calls accursed.

The community of Christians that stayed on in Jerusalem after the ascension must have been forced to deal with this issue in an acute way, since they lived where the crucifixion happened. Perhaps Mark's interpretations reflect much of their thought and teaching on the subject. That being the case, Jerusalem would have been the place where Christians collected memories of Jesus' trial and death and passages from the Hebrew Scriptures that were understood as prophecies of these events.

This community centered around the Twelve at first, and Peter was at the head of it. Later, though, James, the brother of Jesus, seems to have been in charge. Both Acts and Paul's statements in Galatians give the impression that this Jerusalem community was also deeply engaged in controversy with the local Jewish leaders over the correct interpretation of the Torah. Thus the Jerusalem Christian community may also have collected and passed on sayings of Jesus that had to do with Torah observance, sayings that often took the form of: "You have heard it said of old . . . but I say unto you. . . ."

Not all of the Christians in Palestine were in Jerusalem. There appear to have been groups in Galilee that remembered Jesus' ministry among them, and they seem to have developed their own characteristic collections of material about Jesus, mainly sayings. The discussion of that, however, will be postponed until the next section, which will deal with the sayings collection used by Matthew and Luke.

Christian communities sprung up outside Palestine at very early dates. When Paul was converted within a few years of the crucifixion, he found Christians in Damascus. About three years after that he went to Antioch in Syria. Acts says that this was one of a number of places to which the church had spread as a result of persecution in Jerusalem (Acts 11:19-26). The church at Antioch seems to have been started by Greek-speaking Jewish Christians who were less concerned with Torah observance than was the Hebrew-speaking church at Jerusalem. Antioch, therefore, appears to have been one of the first places where it was recognized that a gentile did not have to become a Jew to become a Christian. Paul's missionary activity grew out of that recognition. While Antioch was in Semitic territory, where Judaism was strong, it was a large Hellenistic city, and much of the growth of the Christian community there was among its gentile population. In order to spread the gospel to this new constituency, it was necessary for the Antioch evangelists to state their message in a religious vocabulary that was understood by the people. Since one of the most influential types of religious leader in that area was the miracle worker, it may have been there that collections of stories about the miracles of Jesus began to be made.

Far too little evidence has survived to furnish a detailed picture of how the early Christian community collected and passed on the stories and sayings of Jesus, but the basic situation seems to have been that different centers made, at the least, the following collections of material: (1) an interpretation of the death of Jesus in the light of what were considered predictions in the Hebrew Scriptures, (2) sayings of Jesus about the interpretation of the Torah, (3) other sayings of Jesus, and (4) miracle stories about him.

A Community That Collected Sayings

For a long time, New Testament scholars have assumed that the book of Mark is the oldest written Gospel and that Matthew and Luke had copies of Mark open before them while they wrote. Scholars have also assumed that Matthew and Luke had another source in common, mainly a collection of sayings attributed to Jesus. This collection consists of about two hundred verses that are virtually identical in the two Gospels and of another fifty or so verses that are not so similar but are obviously the same material. This has led the scholars to conclude that the source was written; how otherwise could so much nearly identical wording be accounted for? And it must have been written in Greek rather than in the Aramaic in which Jesus' words were originally spoken, since a written source in Aramaic would not have produced identical translations in the Greek in which Matthew and Luke wrote. Yet they must not have used the same edition of the collection because one-fifth of the total shows marked differences (although there are other explanations for some of these differences). This collection of sayings material, which is called *Q* from the German word *Quelle* (source), amounts to a fourth of the total number of verses in Matthew and somewhere between a fourth and a fifth of Luke. Thus it is a significant part of the whole. It contains some of the teaching of John the Baptist, the three-temptation form of the story of Jesus' testing by Satan, the material in Matthew's Sermon on the Mount and Luke's Sermon on the Plain, the healing of the centurion's son, the missionary charge to Jesus' disciples, some sayings of Jesus about John the Baptist, other sayings about the Pharisees, and sayings about the appearing of the Son of Man.

If these sayings of Jesus are examined for their theological content without reference to the rest of Matthew and Luke, it will be discovered that they have their own themes and emphases. Their main concern is with the immediate coming in glory of the Son of Man to judge the world. They are filled with warnings about how bad that will be for those who have not accepted what they have been taught about Jesus. The Son of Man will give them the same response that they gave the messengers about Jesus.

All of this sounds as though the collection was made by a Christian community in Palestine that had little tie with the Twelve and Jerusalem. They seem to be followers of those who heard Jesus in Galilee and who carry on his work in that area. Having no contact with the leaders in Jerusalem, they seem to get along without other officials except for members who speak ecstatically like prophets. The presence of the risen Lord in their midst seems so real that they do not distinguish sharply between what Jesus said during his earthly ministry and what he said to them after the resurrection through these prophets. Their words have to be accepted as being on a par with his. These prophets probably had the same sort of itinerate ministry that Jesus had known and thus they were equally cut off from home, family, and material goods. They felt a compulsion to preach the news that the Son of Man was coming soon in order to include as many as possible in the blessings of that event. The basis for inclusion was (a) acceptance of the message and (b) living with others in such a way that the reign of God would be obvious.

The community that produced *Q* faded from history by the time of the Jewish-Roman war (A.D. 66–70). Thus they were in existence only a little over thirty years. Yet, they did preserve genuine sayings of Jesus and produce others as a result of their experience of the risen Lord, sayings that have come down through Matthew and Luke as some of the most priceless treasures of the Christian church. This, however, was not their only effect on church history. Their collection had the form of other collections of sayings of the sages, such as the eighth chapter of Proverbs and the section of the Talmud called "sayings of the fathers" (Hebrew: *Pirke Aboth*). This form was also followed by early Christian heretical sects known as Gnostics, who produced such writings as the recently discovered Gospel of Thomas. These latter writings demonstrate the danger of treating what later prophets say in ecstasy as being on a par with what Jesus said during his ministry: any statement one would care to make can be treated as divine revelation. The tendency represented in *Q*, then, could have bad effects if taken to extremes, but, as things are, contemporary Christians have cause for deep gratitude to the community that produced *Q*.

As indicated above, at some point along the way this collection of the sayings of Jesus got written down, and the church's oral tradition about Jesus began to solidify into written form. Before that process of gospel formation can be considered, however, it is necessary to look at the first major production of Christian literature that has survived in more or less the form in which it was written, the letters of Paul.

THINGS TO THINK ABOUT

1. Have you ever thought about an oral stage of transmission of tradition about Jesus that preceded the time the Gospels were written? Does this knowledge change the way you look at biblical books?

2. Does your impression of the Jesus movement change when you think of it as a reform movement among others responding to the crisis of the times? How?

3. Reflect on the fact that different early Christian communities preserved different kinds of information about Jesus.

4. What are the advantages and disadvantages of treating words spoken in ecstasy by early Christian prophets as words of Jesus?

CHAPTER

THREE

The Church Learns to Write

The letters of Paul are addressed to the Christian inhabitants of the cities or regions in which he founded churches. Thus to find the names of those cities, all one has to do is take away the "(i)ans" ending from the title of the letter and replace it with an ending appropriate for a city name: Rome, Corinth, Galatia, Philippi, and Thessalonica. (This list omits Philemon—Paul's one letter to an individual—and letters attributed to Paul that seem to have been written by someone else. More of all that later.) With the exception of Rome, these all sound so much like "faraway places with strange-sounding names" that one could wonder why anyone would ever start a church there.

Yet doing so obviously worked. One of the most remarkable facts of history is the rapidity of the spread of the Christian gospel and church. In the discussion in the previous chapter about places where material about Jesus was preserved, it was seen how quickly the Christian community spread beyond the borders of Palestine. How far and how fast it spread can be illustrated by a couple of incidents. Both relate to the city of Rome, which was the hub of the civilized world of that time. One occurred about twenty years after the death of Jesus. Our record of it comes from the Roman historian and gossip Suetonius: "Since the Jews constantly made disturbances at the instigation of

Chrestus, [the emperor Claudius] expelled them from Rome." Chrestus was a common name at the time, but it could be a misunderstanding of the Latin word for Christ. In that case, it would mean that in this short time Christian missionary activity was already creating such a stir 1,500 miles from Jerusalem that it came to the attention of the Roman emperor (see Acts 18:2).

The other incident has to do with the Emperor Nero and the notorious occasion upon which he was supposed to have fiddled while Rome burned. Nero was rumored to have set the fire to create a dramatic background for his recitation of a poem on the fall of Troy, which, in the manner of the time, was to be accompanied by the lyre. In order to divert suspicion from himself, Nero looked around to find the group in Roman society at the time on which public paranoia focused, the ancient equivalent of "the Red menace," about which the people seemed most willing to believe anything, however horrible. The group that he chose was the Christians. Therefore, less than thirty-five years after the crucifixion, Christians were so well known in the Roman capital that the masses could project their anxieties onto them. Some very effective missionary work had been going on.

The evangelization of Rome and many other important centers was done by anonymous people before Paul came on the scene. Yet it is because his own work is so well documented that we have an idea of the missionary strategies that were pursued. They were very effective. This can be seen, among other places, in Paul's choice of the cities in which he would try to establish churches. As unfamiliar as the names and histories of these cities may be today, no modern sales manager could have chosen better centers for opening up vast new territories.

Corinth is on a four-mile-wide isthmus that connects northern and southern Greece. Since ancient sailors feared open waters and thus skirted coasts, Corinth was more important to shipping in those days than the Panama Canal is now. Any movement popular at Corinth could quickly spread throughout the known world. Even today Thessalonica (long called Salonica) is the second-largest city in Greece. Philippi was on the great Roman highway at the head of the land bridge that connects Greece with Asia Minor (what is modern Turkey). The early church had its greatest growth in Asia Minor, and Ephesus was a gateway into its interior. Galatia was a region of central Asia Minor that included the ancient city that has evolved into Ankara, the capital of modern Turkey. The Pauline mission cities were perfectly positioned for establishing centers for missionary expansion.

Paul's Missionary Strategy

The New Testament provides more information about Paul than about anyone else connected with the early church other than Jesus. Almost half of its books are ascribed to him, and his work occupies the latter half of Acts. Yet less is known about him than might be expected. Many questions of contemporary biographical curiosity are never addressed, the autobiographical sections of his own writings are few and confined to particular details, and some of the information in Acts is inconsistent with what Paul himself wrote, thus leaving questions about the accuracy of data in Acts for which there is no parallel account in Paul's letters.

Paul himself gives no information about his early life other than his saying that he was "circumcised on the eighth day, of the people of Israel, of the tribe of Benjamin, a Hebrew born of Hebrews; as to the law a Pharisee, as to zeal a persecutor of the church, as to righteousness under the law blameless" (Phil. 3:5-6). He does not say that he was born in Tarsus, although he does appear to be a Jew of the

Dispersion into the Greco-Roman world. Nor does he say that he was born a Roman citizen or that his Hebrew name was Saul. He does confess bitterly that he persecuted the church before becoming a Christian, but he does not say where or with what authority. The conversion that Acts describes three times in such detail sounds more like the call of a prophet in his own account of it in Galatians 1:15-16.

Chronological differences also make it difficult to reconcile Acts' long narrative account of Paul's missionary activity with his own statement (Gal. 1:16 2:10). The concern of this book, however, is not the historical reconstruction of the life of Paul, but how Paul came to write to the churches he founded the letters that became the first Christian writings to be preserved and handed down as Holy Scripture. Understanding that requires some knowledge of his missionary methods. Luckily, recent scholarship has made great advances in its understanding of them.

How, then, did Paul go about founding churches in the strategically located cities to which he carried the gospel? Several practical factors were involved. First, the economic base of what he did was his own labor. While he does not say, as Acts does, that he was a tentmaker, he does make it a point of pride that most of the time he was solely responsible for his own support. The term translated "tentmaker" could refer to a variety of occupations, but most scholars now seem to think that Paul was some sort of leather worker. Working as an artisan gave him a portable livelihood, and it also had many advantages for one who was trying to propagate a new system of belief. Contacts with customers could be used for religious talk as well as for transacting business. In the world in which Paul lived there were many traveling advocates of various religions and philosophies. Some supported themselves by begging, others by charging fees, and still others took positions in the households of the wealthy; but quite a number were convinced that supporting themselves was an important demonstration of sincerity. Thus the cities Paul evangelized could fit him into a category of visitors with whom they were familiar.

The next practical factor involved was that Paul knew that in most communities there would be a group of people who were familiar with the categories of thought in which he dealt: members of the local synagogue. It has been estimated that by the time of Paul, Jews composed 7.5 percent of the population of the Roman Empire. There must have been more Jews living outside of Palestine than in it. The story of Pentecost in the book of Acts lists countries from which pilgrims had returned for the feast, and they include most of the known world at the time (2:9-11).

The significance of having Jews everywhere is not limited to the Jews themselves. Many of the nobler pagans found Judaism very attractive. From the perspective of their polytheistic civic religions, the Jewish concept of only one God—a God who was purely spiritual and thus incapable of being depicted visibly by a statue, an "idol"—had a lot to be said for it. Their philosophy had been moving toward such a concept for some time. It had also urged upon them the idea that the moral behavior of a divine being ought to be superior to that of humans, a principle that could not be established by reading about their own gods in the works of Homer. Therefore, many people found the worship of the synagogue very appealing. But they could not cast their lot completely with Judaism without cutting themselves off from all their own people. The dietary laws would have made it impossible for them to eat with their pagan friends and relatives. Even circumcision, the nearest equivalent to baptism, carried with it serious social consequences. Such a mark of Judaism could not go unnoticed in a society in which nude bathing was a standard social activity. Christianity would pose its own discontinuities between its adherents and the population at large, but they were not so radical as these. Synagogues, then, offered missionaries access to people who were yearning to be able to worship the one, true, invisible, moral God without having to turn their backs on all their former associations.

The third practical factor in Paul's missionary method is referred to by the term *house churches*. One thing needed by the early Christian communities founded by Paul and others was a place to meet. The oldest surviving building used exclusively as a church was destroyed in A.D. 256. Since it had not been used as a church all that long before it was destroyed, having their own building was obviously not an option for Paul's churches two centuries earlier. Another way to get a meeting place would be to rent a hall of some sort, and there are indications in the New Testament that this was done on occasion. By far the most common expedient, however, seems to have been to meet in the home of a church member.

In whose home would they meet? Certainly not that of a slave, since slaves had no homes they could call their own, nor in the home of a poor person because there simply would not be room. Passages in Paul's letters suggest that a number of the congregations he founded included some wealthy people who could afford the sort of house that would have ample room for the worshiping community. Scholars have conjectured that many of these may have been freed slaves who had risen to great wealth because of their administrative and other abilities but who nevertheless would always have had an inferior status in class-conscious Roman society.

The Christian gospel of God's love for all would have offered these people an acceptance that they did not find elsewhere. They, in turn, had much to give these young churches in addition to a place to meet. They could provide security, both financial and judicial, and they could also provide leadership when Paul was not around. Not all aspects of their membership were beneficial, though, as Paul suggests in I Corinthians 11, where he talks about wealthy members of the congregation turning the supper in connection with the eucharist into a time of banqueting and wine for themselves while they excluded the poorer members of the congregation.

These three factors, then, of Paul's self-support as an artisan, his building on the foundation of the synagogues, and his use of house churches made it possible for him to have a good base in each place for building a Christian community.

Apostle by Epistle

The strategy outlined above would have been very effective when Paul was present, but what about when he had a congregation well launched and had moved on to start another elsewhere? Partly he managed by return visits, but he could not be everywhere at once. The rest of the time he managed either by the use of representatives or by letter writing or by both. The letters, of course, are what have survived, and most of what is known about the early spread of Christianity is learned from them.

It may be surprising to many people that there were letters in those days. Mail as it is known today seems such a modern thing. Obviously it was not air mail nor was it even carried by trains or trucks. Was there a postal service? Who delivered mail? What were letters written on? What did people write about? Were their letters like ours?

The answers to these and many more questions have been learned since the beginning of this century. There was no government or even private postal service for the public at large, although the Roman Empire had an extensive governmental bureaucracy that carried on a great deal of official correspondence. The empire was crisscrossed by a network of excellent roads that not only permitted the efficient transfer of troops but also made it possible for emergency messages to proceed from one end of the empire to the other with incredible speed through a system not unlike America's Pony Express.

That system, however, was for government use only. Ordinary people had their letters carried for them either by messengers they sent for the purpose or by people they knew were going in that direction. Travel, however, was very slow. While the wealthy could afford horses and even carriages of a sort, most people could not. For long distances the fastest means of transportation was by water, but, as noted above, these vessels hugged the coastlines rather than risking the open sea. The only propulsion they had was what wind gave to sails or slaves gave to oars. And there were seasons when ships did not go to sea. This means that most letters were carried by people on foot.

Many thousands of letters have come down from the period of the New Testament. Most of them have come from Egypt, where the aridity of the climate has retarded the decay of organic matter. These Egyptian letters were, for the most part, written on papyrus, a paperlike material made from the pulp of reeds. Others, though, were written on bits of broken pottery called *ostraka*. In those days when storage, cooking, and eating vessels were made of baked clay, one of the most common waste materials was sherds of broken pottery. Many of these were large enough to write on; sherds have been found with such things as school exercises and letters written on them. The English word *ostracism* is derived from a Greek word that means to write on a sherd a vote to exile someone from the community. Even the largest ostrakon could hold only so much writing, though, so all of the letters of Paul that have come down to us must have been written on long rolls of papyrus by the person to whom he was dictating.

The purposes for which people wrote letters in the ancient world were about as numerous as they are today—although they were not always the same purposes. Separated members of a family wrote to one another, as did friends. Much business was transacted through correspondence, at times adding little more than a salutation and closing greeting to a legal document. Some friendly letters were highly polished literary works that were intended for publication. Philosophers used letters to do what today would be called the "spiritual direction" of their followers. These letters are probably more like the letters of Paul than any others from his time. His, however, were not addressed to individuals but to communities, and they deal not with efforts at self improvement but with community efforts to obey the will of God.

Letters then as now had fixed forms that were followed. A letter would begin with the name of the sender and the name of the recipient followed by a salutation: "Publius to his father and mother, greetings." Sometimes this would be expanded to include titles or terms of affection or geographical locations. This was normally followed by some form of well wishing, such as: "If you are well, it would be excellent. I too am well." And, since even many of the pagans were very devout, there would often be a prayer, especially a thanksgiving. At the end would be a short closing. The form of the body of the letter would be determined by its subject and purpose. Paul's letters incorporated Christian adaptations of these forms, as may be seen from the first few verses of I Corinthians:

Paul, called by the will of God to be an apostle of Christ Jesus, and our brother Sosthenes, To the church of God which is at Corinth, to those sanctified in Christ Jesus, called to be saints together with all those who in every place call on the name of our Lord Jesus Christ, both their Lord and ours: Grace to you and peace from God our Father and from the Lord Jesus Christ. I give thanks to God always for you.

The next two chapters will be devoted to the individual letters. The purpose of this one has been to show how letters came to be an important part of the strategy of the early Christian missionary movement. As noted above, for Paul the letters were his third best way of dealing with a crisis in one of his churches. If he could, he would go in person. If he could not, his first choice was to send a trusted representative. But if he could not do that, he would write a letter. This means that he had no idea when he began to dictate a letter that it would later be regarded by the church as being on a level of inspiration with the Hebrew Scriptures. He must have regarded what he was doing as much more on the order of plugging a leak in a dam until something more lasting could be done about it. But the Holy Spirit often accomplishes through the people of God far better things than they could ever imagine are being done.

THINGS TO THINK ABOUT

1. Did you know that the early Christian movement spread so rapidly? What is your reaction to this insight?
2. Do you think Paul's method of spreading the gospel would work today? Why or why not?
3. How do you react to the idea that Paul's letters were not written as scripture?
4. How does knowledge of ancient letter writing contribute to your understanding of Paul's missionary activity?

C H A P T E R
F O U R

Letters to the Family

Among the many metaphors Paul used to express his understanding of the church, none seemed to come to him more naturally than that of the family or household. The family he had in mind, of course, was not the intimate nuclear family of today but the much more inclusive ancient Roman household. This was a wider concept that was more intergenerational than the modern understanding, one that included servants and slaves and even business partners. This metaphor of family enabled Paul to address the recipients of his letters as "brothers and sisters," although at other times he took a more paternal stance. And he was even able to use feminine figures of speech, referring to himself as their mother (Gal. 4:19) or tenderly caring nurse (I Thess. 2:7). There are also a number of places where the figure of business partner is invoked.

All of this gives a special personal quality, an air of family letters, to Paul's correspondence. This is not to say that Paul's attitude toward his addressees is always positive; the relation is too much like that of real families for negative emotions to be entirely absent. But the emotional tone is always that of people who are deeply involved with one another. In this chapter, a short look will be taken at some of the letters that modern scholars think Paul himself wrote.

Thus it will be possible to note the different ways he expressed his family feeling toward his congregations.

The Earliest Letter

Scholars generally agree that the oldest surviving letter written by Paul is I Thessalonians. It is impossible to tell whether he wrote others earlier that have not been preserved or whether this was the first. If Acts gives a correct impression of where the foundation of the church at Thessalonica fits into the missionary career of Paul (near the beginning of the so-called Second Missionary Journey), it makes sense to think of writing as an appropriate new apostolic tool for Paul as he began a new stage of his ministry, one in which he would have responsibility for a number of widely separated congregations. Yet Acts 17:1-10 does not depict the situation in Thessalonica as being in every way the same as it is reflected in the letter. Acts, for instance, suggests only a three-week stay, but I Thessalonians says that Paul worked to support himself while he was there (2:9) and gives the impression of a thoroughly organized congregation (5:12-13). Paul also says in his letter to the Philippians that they had sent him gifts twice while he was in Thessalonica. All of this suggests a much longer stay than three weeks. Still, the sequence of periods of activity in Acts could be right even if the length of all the periods is not correct.

This theory of letter writing as a tool for apostolic ministry may account for Paul's beginning to write at all, but why did he write this particular letter? One place that some scholars have looked for an explanation is I Thessalonians 2:1-12, in which Paul discusses how he and his associates behaved while they were in Corinth. To their minds, these words of Paul sound defensive and suggest that the passage must be a reply to charges made against him. They point out that reading Paul is like hearing one end of a telephone conversation and trying to figure out what is being said on the other end.

This analogy is not encouraging, however. On the one hand, most efforts to make such deductions have not been very successful. On the other, the use of such an analogy is a reminder of how different our technological age is from Paul's time.

Paul's words may sound defensive to an age that is inclined to give all human behavior a psychological explanation, but they would have sounded very different to an age in which most education was in public speaking, or, as it was called, rhetoric.

The authors of textbooks on rhetoric gave elaborate rules for presenting any kind of argument, but they recognized three main kinds of proof that they called *ethos* (the trustworthiness of the speaker), *logos* (the use of reason), and *pathos* (an appeal to the emotions). Several types of speeches called especially for the establishment of the trustworthiness of the speaker. Among these were speeches to urge the audience to higher standards of behavior. Although it would sound immodest today, it was common then for those making such speeches to offer their own behavior as a model for imitation. That is what Paul seems to have been doing in 2:1-12, which suggests that his purpose was to spur the Thessalonian Christians on to greater virtue.

Saying that his purpose was moral exhortation, however, is not to suggest that Paul was dissatisfied with his newly founded Christian community. The whole letter breathes his love and gratitude for them. Expanding on the classical formula for letter writing, he followed the convention of having a thanksgiving come right after the greeting of all of his letters but one, but the thanksgiving in this letter is the longest he wrote.

The occasion for Paul's writing to the Thessalonians

comes out in chapter 3: they have "suffered affliction." It may be that they have been persecuted (see 2:13-16, although some scholars regard these verses as the addition of a later hand). At any rate, Paul sent Timothy to find out how they had borne up under this affliction, and Timothy returned with a glowing report. Paul wrote to express his gratitude, but he also had another purpose in mind. He had learned, perhaps from Timothy, that the Thessalonians were concerned about the fate of their Christian dead. Perhaps they had expected none of their members to die before the return of Christ. Either Paul had not had an opportunity to instruct them on this subject or they had misunderstood what he had said. Now, at any rate, he was able to set them straight and to fill them with hope. Thus he was able to use a letter to encourage them in a time of doubt when he had to be physically absent.

This first letter of Paul to a branch of his Christian family, then, seems to have been written both to express his joy that they had stood up so well under affliction and to straighten out their thoughts about the fate of their Christian dead. Yet, always the good teacher and preacher, he did not pass up the opportunity the letter gave to exhort them to even higher standards of Christian behavior.

A Reproclamation of Emancipation

The second letter of Paul to a branch of his Christian family to have been preserved, far from expressing his satisfaction with the progress of the group, shows deep alarm over the possibility of their turning their backs on everything he had taught them. This letter, then, begins very abruptly; it does not have the thanksgiving that is characteristic of all of Paul's other letters. It is full of sarcasm and insults, and at one point Paul calls his addressees "foolish Galatians" (Gal. 3:1). While the traditional way of interpreting all of this has been to see such expressions as indications of Paul's strong emotions while writing, there is reason to believe that J. B. Phillips may have caught Paul's tone better when he paraphrased this address as "O you dear idiots of Galatia."

Here again reference must be made to the rhetorical conventions of Paul's day. Compositions have come down from classical antiquity that have all the verve and apparent venom of Galatians, indicating that strong expressions—far from being an indication of the emotional state of the speaker or writer—may indeed represent close attention to the literary pattern of certain kinds of writing. Rather than indications of the heat of the moment, they may be signs of the careful observation of literary conventions. Certainly Galatians is argued tightly enough to lend credence to the assumption that it was not rapidly dashed off in a fit of temper.

To understand what Paul was trying to accomplish in this document, however, it is necessary to get some sense of who the Galatian Christians were and why Paul may have wished to write so strong a letter to them. Galatia refers to the territory in the middle of what is now Turkey, which comprised an ancient kingdom that had been settled by relatives of the Gallic/Celtic peoples who inhabited much of what is now France and Britain. By the time of Paul, though, these people had intermarried with the indigenous people and had in turn been incorporated into Greek and Roman provinces, adopting the culture of their conquerors but remaining away from the centers of those cultures. Nothing is known of the exact ethnic mix of the members of Paul's churches, but Hans Dieter Betz is undoubtedly right in saying that their cultural status would have been that of "hicks," persons excluded from the mainstream.

Their Christian conversion, therefore, would have had the effect of not only conferring its religious benefits but also communicating with them a sense of well-being that would have overcome any negative effects of their social position. In every way, then, becoming Christians must have been a liberating experience for them. Furthermore, since I Corinthians makes it very clear that ecstatic religious experience was a characteristic of at least some of the congregations Paul founded, the Galatian Christians may also have had that heady experience.

The letter suggests, though, that that phenomenon may have run its course—just as it has in some contemporary congregations that have been a part of the charismatic renewal movement. Sometimes it happens that churches that seemed filled with the Spirit just sort of run down. That time is occasionally hastened by the discovery that some of those who seem most filled with the Spirit are still quite susceptible to temptation and fall into sin in ways that are embarrassingly public. That seems to be what happened in Galatia.

At about the time that disillusionment was setting in, there appeared in the Galatian churches another group of Christian missionaries who represented a tradition different from that of Paul. They still believed that in order to become Christian one must first become a Jew, accepting the burden of circumcision and other obligations of the Torah. Their explanation for the failure of the Galatians to live without sin is that they had no right to expect to because they were not keeping the explicit commandments of God's Law.

This argument seems to have been entirely persuasive to the Galatian Christians, and word of that got back to Paul. He considered the position disastrous and wrote this letter to help them understand why. Recently Hans Dieter Betz, referred to above, has argued very strongly that, to make his letter as persuasive as possible, Paul borrowed a literary form from classical rhetoric, the form of an apologetic letter. Classical rhetoric did not give nearly as much attention to letter writing (or any other kind of writing) as it did to public speaking, and many of the forms of written composition developed were based on speech forms. Three main kinds of speeches were recognized: judicial (used for pleading one's case in court), deliberative (used in legislative bodies to decide what ought to be done) and epideictic (used on ceremonial occasions to praise or blame someone or something). Since the apologetic letter is written to defend oneself (not to say that one is sorry for having done something), its functions were very much like those of a judicial speech of defense; therefore, the letter takes on the essential outline of such a speech.

A judicial speech begins with an introduction *(exordium)* to get the favorable attention of the court. It moves from a summary of the events to be interpreted by the court *(narratio)*, to a statement of one's case *(propositio)*, to an effort to prove that case positively and negatively *(probatio)*. The speech ends with an emotional appeal to the judges to render the justice requested *(conclusio)*. To adapt this outline for an apologetic letter, all that is necessary is to add an opening greeting to the beginning and a closing salutation to the end, with an exhortation *(exhortatio)* before the conclusion, urging behavior in conformity to one's recommendation. Betz has outlined Galatians as an apologetic letter in this way:

Epistolary prescript 1:1-5
Exordium 1:6-11
Narration 1:12 2:14
Proposition 2:15-21
Proof 3:1 4:31
Exhortation 5:1 6:10
Conclusion 6:11-18

Not all scholars, even among those who use the categories of classical rhetoric, have accepted Betz's analysis of Galatians. Some have suggested that the pattern is not that of a judicial speech but that of a deliberative speech; it is not so much concerned with defending something that happened in the past as it is with urging a pattern of behavior for the future. In any case, critics of rhetoric have caused it to be recognized that Galatians is a carefully considered and constructed piece of argumentative prose rather than something dashed off in the heat of the moment. It is a tightly woven demonstration that the temptation to take on the burden of legal observance will not restore the freedom of the spirit the Galatians have lost. Rather, as Betz says, "freedom exists only in so far as people live in freedom" (see Dieter Betz, *Galatians* [Philadelphia: Fortress Press, 1979], p. 32). Thus this epistle is a powerful exhortation "to let the 'fruit of the Spirit' happen," to return to the glorious freedom of the children of God that was made available to all who will accept it by the cross of Jesus Christ. Apparently Paul's argument was persuasive; a year later he wrote to the church at Corinth and told them that the collection he was taking up for the church at Jerusalem was being well supported by the Galatians (I Cor. 16:1).

Family Squabbles

Galatians was written to deal with trouble that had been stirred up by outsiders, but the emergency to which I Corinthians is Paul's response was stirred up entirely within the church family. The letter falls into two parts, with chapters 1–6 constituting Paul's way of dealing with information brought to him by members of the household of Chloe (in whose house the congregation probably met). The rest of the letter was apparently a reply to a series of questions sent to Paul by the congregation through other messengers.

At first the two sections appear to have little to do with one another. Chloe's people have brought Paul news of factionalism in the congregation, while the questions the congregation asks concern practical and moral problems. Yet, closer inspection shows how closely related the issues are. The factions seem to be related to who baptized whom, with the implication that those who were baptized by one person were superior to those baptized by another. The questions submitted by the Corinthians all relate in one way or another to issues of superiority. Some of the members of the congregation seem to have a special capacity for ecstatic phenomena, such as speaking in tongues. These abilities, which appear to be associated with baptism by certain people, are thought to elevate those who have them beyond all ordinary obligations. The varieties of sexual behavior in the congregation, for instance, suggest that a successful soap opera could be written about what went on. (Perhaps it could be called "Isthmian Games" in a play on the name of famous athletic contests held near Corinth.)

Those who had these religious experiences claimed that through them they received supernatural knowledge. This claim makes them sound like heretics of a kind who flourished a century later—the Gnostics. *Gnostic* is derived from the Greek word for knowledge and refers to the claim of its adherents that they were saved through knowledge they possessed, the knowledge that the body and even the material universe was not their home. Rather, their spirits were flecks of the very essence of God that had somehow become separated and exiled upon earth. Their salvation consisted in their learning of their heavenly origin, which freed them to return to their home in the being of God.

While there are similarities in the claims to knowledge and in the sense of superiority that raised one above the ordinary obligations of life, the Corinthian ecstatic group does not seem to have developed the belief in heavenly origin that is essential to full-scale Gnosticism. Their claim to superiority is based instead on their religious experiences.

Paul's consistently argued position, whether he is

dealing with it at a theoretical level in the first six chapters or applying it to practical questions in the rest of the letter, is his insistence that any claim to superiority in the Christian community is a contradiction in terms, since nothing is more contrary to the spirit of Christ than the desire to be better than other people or to have an advantage over them. The definitive Christian virtue is not spirituality but love. This love must extend to all other members of the community and even beyond that to embrace the whole human race. Thus logically as well as literarily and spiritually, the climax of I Corinthians is the rhapsody on love that makes up the thirteenth chapter. But even the exaltation of this superlative virtue is not the end of the matter; the real point is that the cross of Christ is the standard against which all human behavior is to be measured. It is the only criterion against which anything can be said to be good. The irony built into this principle is that any claim to superiority is prima facie evidence that one does not possess it. But anything less than this Christian love is "a noisy gong or a clanging cymbal."

This is the way that Paul responded to the crisis at Corinth in his letter, which is all there is room to discuss in this book. Yet because of the practical issues dealt with in it, I Corinthians offers the best insight available into the world in which the early church lived. It is to be hoped that readers will be able to learn more about that through other studies they make of this letter.

A Family Letter of Recommendation

The extent to which Paul was governed in his thinking about the church by the metaphor of family comes out clearly in the shortest, most personal, and most charming of his letters, that to Philemon. But even this is not completely a private letter; it is also addressed to "Apphia our sister and Archippus our fellow soldier, and the church at your house." Nevertheless most of it addresses Philemon in the second person singular. The letter was written to return to Philemon a runaway slave, Onesimus. But family relations have changed since Onesimus left. He met Paul in prison; whether he was a fellow prisoner or sought Paul out is not known. Staying in jail was not a punishment in the ancient world, and prisoners could have visitors—indeed, they needed them to supply food and other necessities. Paul says that Onesimus was born to him in prison and thus calls him his son. This probably means that Onesimus became a Christian then, but Paul is not less serious in describing the relation that way because of this religious dimension. Onesimus, though, is not the only one to whom Paul has a special relation; Philemon owes Paul his very self (v. 19). The similarity of the relations of Philemon and Onesimus to Paul has implications for their relation to one another: Paul urges Philemon to take Onesimus back "no longer as a slave but more than a slave, as a beloved brother"(v. 16).

Does this mean that Paul wanted Philemon to accept Onesimus back as a slave without punishing him for running away or that Paul wanted Philemon to free Onesimus? Probably the latter, although Paul refrains from saying what he wants, relying on Philemon's good will and gratitude to him. Paul does say strongly, however, that Onesimus is very helpful to him, and one gets the idea that what Paul would like best is for Philemon to send Onesimus to assist him in his ministry.

The essential form of the letter is that of a letter of recommendation, a type of which many examples have been preserved from the period. There is even one from Pliny, a well-known literary letter writer, asking a friend to forgive a runaway servant. But no one else suggests that a slave be treated as an equal and a member of the family. Paul saw the gospel as radically transforming all human relations.

THINGS TO THINK ABOUT

1. How do you react to Paul's metaphor of family to describe the congregation? Would you like to see revived the old custom of church members addressing one another as "brother" and "sister"?

2. How do you feel about the expectations of Paul and other early Christians that the second coming of Christ and the end of the world would be in their lifetime?

3. Can you think of situations in the life of the church today in which the considerations raised by Paul in Galatians would be important?

4. How do Paul's reflections about factions in the church at Corinth illuminate situations in congregations today?

5. Does it disturb you that Paul does not directly attack the institution of slavery? Do you think that his anticipation that the world would end soon was involved in that failure? Explain.

C H A P T E R
F I V E

Repackaged Mail

Occasionally someone receives something from the post office that has been stamped to indicate that its original wrapping had begun to come apart in transit and thus had been repaired or replaced. The contents of such parcels are not always still in the condition in which they were mailed. Sometimes it is clear that things have been mixed up if not damaged in shipping. Some of Paul's letters seem to New Testament scholars to have undergone similar fates. There is no doubt that he wrote what is there, but something seems to have happened to it since he finished with it. Parts appear to be no longer in the place where they started out. The feeling is similar to that stated by an English theologian of a mistaken view of the resurrection of the body expected by Christians, a view in which one could expect to say something like, "Oh yes, this bit used to be over there."

These scholarly theories usually take the form of considering an epistle of Paul as it appears in the New Testament to be not one letter but a composite of several letters or parts of letters. The issue is not the *authenticity* of the letter (whether Paul wrote it) but its *integrity* (whether it was originally one document). Of course, these theories are exactly that: theories. Their only validity comes from their superior ability to account for the evidence, the material in the New Testament and its arrangement. Thus rather than arguing about whether such rearrangements of the text are likely or not, it seems better to look at the epistles whose integrity has been questioned to see if that theory makes more sense than saying that Paul wrote them just as they appear in the Bible today. This chapter, therefore, will be concerned not only with how Paul came to write but also with how somebody else came to fuse—how Holy Writ was written *in the form in which we find it.* Needless to say, claiming that several letters have been edited into one does not bring their inspiration into question. God could have inspired those who edited them as well as the original writer.

The Corinthian File

The place to begin in considering whether II Corinthians was originally several letters rather than just one is with the fact that Paul wrote more letters to the church at Corinth than have survived. There is a reference to a letter previously written in I Corinthians (5:9). There is also explicit evidence outside the New Testament that collections of correspondence were sometimes shortened by joining a number of letters together, using only the first opening greeting and the last closing salutation but including the full text of everything else. Thus the theory is not fabricated out of whole cloth; such things happened.

What makes the theory really persuasive, though, is the way that so much of the material in II Corinthians does not fit together. To begin with, the first seven chapters express a good bit of gratitude for the reestablishment of friendly relations between Paul and the Corinthian Christians, the next two are about the collection Paul is taking for the church at Jerusalem, and the last four are a tirade against the Corinthians. That is to say that chapters 10–13 sound as if the quarrel that had been patched up in 1–7 is being reopened in the very letter that was written to give thanks that it had been settled. Traditionally this disjuncture has been accounted for by saying that Paul had a bad night's sleep after writing 1–7 and that is reflected in what he wrote the next day or, alternatively, that after he had written 1–7 he had received another message from Corinth, suggesting that things were not going as well as he had thought. But, in either case, if he had changed his mind, why did he send what he had written first, which was in so little accord with his changed feelings? Why not start over?

This question is sharpened when one notices references in chapter 2 to an earlier letter, one that is obviously neither I Corinthians nor the other letter mentioned in it. Paul says that the letter was written "out of much affliction and anguish of heart and with many tears, not to cause you pain but to let you know the abundant love that I have for you" (II Cor. 2:4). The letter may not have been written to cause pain, but Paul goes on in the next verse to make it very clear that he is aware that it could have caused pain. Now the only block of material in the surviving parts of the Corinthian correspondence that tallies with this description is chapters 10–13 of II Corinthians. Is it more likely that the dramatic change of tone between 1–7 and 10–13 is to be accounted for by Paul's changing his mind some way or by some later editor's joining the "painful letter" on to the end of 1–7 (with the two chapters on the collection for the Jerusalem church stuck in between)?

Once one begins to ask this sort of question, others arise immediately. Other disjunctures are noted. For instance, 2:12,13 read as follows: "When I came to Troas to preach the gospel of Christ, a door was opened to me in the Lord, but I did not rest because I did not find my brother Titus there. So I took leave of them and went to Macedonia." At that point, though, Paul's account of his travels is interrupted by a defense of his apostleship that lasts for over five chapters. Then it picks up again in 7:5: "For when we came to

Macedonia, our bodies had no rest but we were afflicted at every turn." Then the next ten verses complete the narrative. It is possible, of course, that Paul digressed here but eventually returned to his point. He can be seen to digress elsewhere in his letters, but for five chapters? That is almost like Oliver Wendell Holmes who interrupted his writing of *The Autocrat of the Breakfast Table* for twenty-five years and resumed at the end of that time with the words, "as we were saying." Possibly the five-chapter defense of Paul's apostleship also comes from a different letter and was inserted into this account of Paul's travels by the later editor.

That still does not solve all of the problems. Second Corinthians 6:14–7:1 interrupts Paul's defense of his apostleship with a warning against Christians associating with pagans that has nothing to do with what comes before it or after it. Rather, 6:13 ends with Paul's calling on the Corinthians to "widen (their) hearts" while 7:2 says: "Open your hearts to us." Thus 6:14–7:1 has nothing to do with its surrounding passages and interrupts what would have been a smooth flow. Not only that, scholars who have made a close study of Paul's language and thought say that these verses do not even sound like something written by Paul. Thus they conjecture that the editor picked up these alien verses from some other author entirely and stuck them in here for reasons that must have seemed adequate at the time but which are incomprehensible today.

Only one other bit of data is needed to complete this survey of the discontinuities in II Corinthians. It has to do with chapters 8 and 9, the two that deal with Paul's collection for the Jerusalem church. Not only do they not have much to do with what comes before or after them, but the two do not seem a part of the same discussion of the collection as well. Possibly each of them was originally separate or a part of some other document. But if the theory is true that II Corinthians is made up of some six letters in whole or in part, what sense can be made of how Paul came to write all of these letters? As a matter of fact, it can all be fitted into a reasonable pattern that is consistent with the autobiographical statements from Paul that are scattered through. First of all, 6:14–7:1 is to be discarded (not from the Bible but from this reconstruction) because Paul did not write it. His first letter after I Corinthians would be 2:14–7:4 (with 6:14–7:1 omitted, of course). He has heard that outsiders have come in with impressive credentials to undermine his teaching, but he does not yet take this opposition seriously enough, and so the letter fails in its purpose of reestablishing his leadership. When he learns of this result, he decides that the gravity of the situation now requires him to make a visit (2:1). The visit, however, is a total failure, so he goes home to Ephesus and fires off the "painful letter" (chapters 10–13). Then he sends his associate Titus to do what he can to patch things up (the mission that is referred to in the travel narrative interrupted by 2:14–7:4). When he and Titus are reunited, Titus has entirely happy news for him (7:7) and thus he responds with the warm and gracious letter that gives its framework to the epistle as it now exists (1:1–2:13, 7:5-16).

This theory accounts for all of the components of II Corinthians, but what explanation can be offered for why someone would wish to piece them together in this fashion? Any such explanation must begin with the fact that II Corinthians was not in circulation at the end of the first century. First Clement, one of the oldest Christian writings outside the New Testament, was written about that time by a leader of the church in Rome to the church in Corinth, and it alludes to I Corinthians as though it were the only letter Paul had written to that church.

One scholar has noted that at the turn of the first century one of the most pressing issues in the church was false teachers. At that time, then, Paul's "painful letter" (II Cor. 10–13) would have sounded like a ringing denunciation of heresiarchs. **Further, his list of his sufferings on behalf of the gospel (11:23 ff.)** would have aligned him with the martyrs—another issue of the time, as the letters of Ignatius of Antioch show. Finally, coming right after 2:14, Paul's travel narrative would not be interpreted as the indecisive movements of an anxious pastor. Who would have thought then that any congregation could have resisted "the apostle to the gentiles"? Rather, it would be understood as Paul's triumphal procession through the world of the gentiles. This combination of the denunciation of heretics, showing Paul as a martyr, and depicting him on a triumphal procession would be an adequate reason to edit this part of the Corinthian correspondence in the way it appears in the New Testament.

Another scholar has offered an even more precise accounting for the editing of the many fragments into II Corinthians. He recognizes that I Clement was written to the church of Corinth because the church at Rome had learned that the elders of the Corinthian church had been ejected by younger members of the congregation. These elders would be the ones who had possession of such treasures of the congregation as letters from Paul. They could have edited those to bring out the parallels between their situation and that of Paul so that his words could be used to condemn their opponents.

Letters and Papers from Prison

The more common scholarly interpretation of Philippians makes it appropriate to borrow for this letter and for the section of this book about it the title given to a collection of works of Dietrich Bonhoeffer, the German theologian who was martyred under Hitler. This view is not shared by all scholars, and it is much harder to reconstruct an exact sequence for the documents enclosed in this epistle than it is for those in II Corinthians. Yet the theory of multiple letters does make sense of what appear to be inconsistencies within Philippians, and so it will be followed here. If the theory is correct, it casts additional light on the way Paul corresponded with his churches, since the impression left would be of a number of short letters rather than a few long ones. Thus the question would be raised again of whether Paul wrote many letters that have not been preserved.

The multiple letters theory would also have implications about where Paul was when he wrote Philippians. He makes it clear that he was in jail; he is known to have been imprisoned in Rome, so some think the epistle must have been written from there. Most, however, think that he wrote from Ephesus, which is much nearer to Philippi, thus making a frequent exchange of messages more feasible. Paul does not mention an imprisonment in Ephesus explicitly, but he was there a long time. He was imprisoned more than once in places that he does not identify, and he does speak of having "fought with the beasts at Ephesus," which may be metaphoric but nevertheless suggests some sort of difficulty there.

The view that Philippians is a composite of several letters holds that 4:10-20 is the first one, a note of thanksgiving for a contribution toward his support from the only congregation that he allowed to assist him in that way. In this "bread and butter" note he makes no mention of being in prison. That is not the case, however, in 1:1–3:1. There the Philippians have responded to news that he was in jail by sending him Epaphroditus. Now, Epaphroditus has become ill, and Paul is sending him back home to them. In this section, he comments on his attitude to being in prison and possibly in danger of death. And, as scholars have noted, it is precisely this letter that is dominated by repeated invitations to joy. The third letter in Philippians (which does not appear to be complete in the present epistle) is 3:2–4:3, which deals with false apostles who have come to

Philippi urging circumcision and Torah observance on the Christians there. The other verses in Philippians are closing greetings, and it is impossible to tell which ones went with which of these letters originally.

Whether originally three letters or one, this is one of the most beloved of Paul's epistles. It is concerned in all its sections with the mutual participation that he and the Philippians have in one another and that they together have in Christ. It contains precious autobiographical information (3:5-6), and it also preserves a wonderful early Christian hymn about the pre-existence of Christ (2:5-11).

A Letter to Strangers

The letter to the Romans, Paul's longest and most important, has been repackaged less than II Corinthians or Philippians. Only the last chapter comes into serious doubt. This chapter (16) seems to be the sort of list of greetings with which Paul usually ends his letters, but the list is very long and Paul had not founded the church in Rome, had not been there, and probably would not have known or known about so many individuals. Further, some of these names are associated with Ephesus. The suggestion has been made, therefore, that the copy of Romans that Paul sent to Rome did not have this final chapter. Instead, an additional copy of this magnum opus was sent to the church at Ephesus, and Paul wrote chapter 16 to personalize it for the Ephesians.

This section also begins with a commendation of Phoebe, a church worker of Cenchreae, the port on the other side of the narrow isthmus from Corinth where Paul wrote this correspondence. It seems that she was going to take up a ministry among those to whom chapter 16 was written. Other women are named in these greetings, which appears to be a list of church workers rather than just ordinary members. Apparently Paul, who has come to have such a reputation as a woman-hater, was much more open to the ministry of women than most Christians since his time have been up until the last few years.

A book devoted to the writing of the New Testament should certainly have something significant to say about what is generally regarded as one of the most important books in the Bible, but in some ways providing that is easier said than done because scholars are a long way from agreeing about why Paul wrote his longest letter to a church where he was unknown. There is some sense, of course, that he wrote it as a letter of self-recommendation to enlist the support of the Roman church, as he was ready to launch out on a new phase of ministry that would take him to Spain.

That alone, however, does not seem to account for so detailed a letter, especially one that has as its subject something that is not too relevant to the Spanish mission—namely, the relative position of Jews and gentiles before God. One thing should be clear, though: the interpretation, traditional since Martin Luther, that sees Romans as concerned with what individuals must do to be saved misses the point. Paul is discussing the relative advantages of two religious communities, not individual spiritual struggles.

But why is he discussing those? He wrote the letter just as he was tying up his ministry in Asia Minor and Greece, to which he had devoted a number of years, and was capping that off by bringing what must have been a very substantial financial offering from his gentile churches to the Jewish church in Jerusalem. That, together with his anxieties about what he would find waiting for him in Jerusalem—anxieties that proved all too well founded—would certainly leave him preoccupied with questions about the relative situation of Jews, gentiles, and Christians before God.

But why write to the Romans about that? It may be that Paul had received information about struggles that were going on in the church(es) of Rome. When the Jews had been driven out of Rome by Claudius around A.D. 49, the gentile Christians had been left on their own for a number of years without direct knowledge of the religious matrix out of which Christianity had been born. It may be that during the years before the Jewish Christians returned, the gentile control over the Christian community had produced a spirit that was very insensitive to Jewish Christian feelings about Torah observance. When the Jewish Christians returned, therefore, they may have felt left out and uncared for. Chapters 14 and 15 have a good bit to say about the "weak" and the "strong" without ever identifying those two groups. Maybe the weak are the Roman Jewish Christians and the strong are the gentile Christians who are inconsiderate of them. Paul, therefore, may have written his masterpiece to help resolve a tension that was tearing apart the church at Rome.

At any rate, Paul did not arrive in Rome the way he had planned. Instead of being a missionary on his way through to Spain, he came as a prisoner to be tried before the Roman emperor. The chances are that he was never released and never got to Spain. Instead, he met a martyr's death in Rome.

THINGS TO THINK ABOUT

1. Does it disturb you to think that several of Paul's letters may have been compressed into one? If so, why? What could be said in favor of this interpretation?

2. Have you known pastors who agonized over their congregations as Paul does in II Corinthians?

3. If the theory of how some of Paul's letters were put together is true, what difference does it make? (This differs from Question 1, which was about how the theory was arrived at, while this has to do with the use to be made of it after it is accepted.)

4. How does the insight that Romans is not about the spiritual struggles of individuals but about the relative status of two religious groups affect our understanding of it?

CHAPTER

SIX

The Difference It Makes

A matter that is disturbing to the faith of some Christians is that many New Testament scholars think that Paul did not write six of the thirteen epistles ascribed to him. To these Christians, that seems to bring into question both the honesty of those who made those attributions and the reliability of the documents themselves as guides for Christian belief and practice.

This attitude is but one of many examples that could be given of the differences between the way people in the world of the New Testament looked at things and the way people today look at them. One of my seminary professors used to refer often to "the difficulties modern occidental people have in reading an ancient oriental book" such as the Bible. Kipling's remark that "East is East and West is West, and never the twain shall meet," has become proverbial wisdom, and it could also be said that "old is old and new is new."

One of the major areas in which attitudes differed is that of the use that one writer could make of the work or name of another writer. Today there are copyright laws to offer protection against plagiarism and forgery, but the attitude behind such laws was missing in the ancient world. If a person was writing a book on a subject and found something good someone else had written about that subject, the writer would feel no hesitation in incorporating it without so much as a footnote, acknowledgment, or by-your-leave. The use of Mark by Matthew and Luke is a case in point from the New Testament.

By the same token, writers felt free to create works that claimed to have been written by someone else. Partly this was a result of the educational system. As has been noted, the basic educational system was training in effective public speaking. One way in which this rhetoric was taught was to have students write speeches in the style of famous orators, just as someone learned to paint by copying the works of the great masters. It would have been as inappropriate to accuse the rhetorical students of forgery as it was to charge the painting students with it.

Further, much of the teaching of philosophical schools was done through letter writing. The philosopher would write a letter of moral or spiritual direction to a disciple, intending both to guide that individual and to publish the letter later in a collection of such letters as part of a treatise on how to live according to the insights of that philosophical school. It was only natural that after the death of the founder the teachings of the school would continue to be developed by successors and equally natural for them to incorporate these developments into the official literature by writing additional letters in the name of the founder.

Something very similar to this practice in Greco-Roman philosophy went on in the circles of the Hebrew prophets. In their lifetimes, the prophets had groups of followers who were called their "school." After a prophet's death, the followers would continue to speak in the prophet's name and add oracles to the collection of the prophet's sayings, which make up the prophetical book in the Hebrew Scriptures called by that prophet's name. In these prophetical schools, this practice was encouraged by an understanding of what has been called "corporate personality."

The group was thought to share one spirit—the spirit of the prophet-founder—so that whatever the group said could be understood as an authentic utterance of the prophet. Thus most of the canonical books of prophecy have some oracles that were uttered posthumously by the prophet's school. The clearest case is the book of Isaiah, which is generally believed to have been written at three different periods (before, during, and after the exile in Babylon). The writers are referred to as Isaiah (chapters 1–39), Second Isaiah (chapters 40–55), and Third Isaiah (chapters 56–66).

The principle is similar to that by which the community who produced the Q document included sayings that they thought the risen Lord had spoken through their prophets along with what Jesus had said during his earthly ministry. Far from considering this practice dishonest, they would have thought omitting these to be an utter denial of the blessing of the divine presence they had experienced in their midst.

This takes care of the issue of honesty, but what about that of reliability, that of religious authority? To answer this question it is necessary to return to the concept of the canon, or authoritative list of books that make up the Christian Scriptures. The biblical authority of a book is not derived from its author but from its being included in the canon.

An extreme example of this principle can be seen in The Gospel of Thomas, a Gnostic collection of sayings of Jesus dating from the middle of the second century that was discovered in Egypt in 1945. It is generally agreed that the collection itself is relatively late and represents the point of view of a heretical sect, so there is no suggestion that the book as a whole should be included in the New Testament. But some very fine scholars think that what Jesus actually said on some occasions is more accurately reflected in passages in The Gospel of Thomas than it is in the form the same saying takes in one of the canonical gospels. And it is also admitted that some sayings in Thomas for which there are no parallels in the canonical gospels may be genuine sayings of Jesus.

If there really are such words of Jesus in this Gnostic document, do they have canonical authority? No! They may have the authority of Jesus, but they do not have the authority of scripture. Scriptural authority as such belongs only to words in the list of books that the Holy Spirit has caused the church to regard as inspired. Thus it can be seen that a letter that claims to have been written by Paul would not lose its position in the canon if it were proved that he did not write it. The authority of the book comes from its place in the canon, not from its authorship. If it were known that a book was written by followers of Paul rather than by Paul himself, the book would remain just as much a part of the New Testament as it ever was and would be just as precious to Christians. The only difference would be that they would know how to interpret it better because they knew the circumstances under which it was written and, therefore, would have better insight into what it was supposed to accomplish.

Letter or Epistle?

So far the only distinction that has been implied by using the word *epistle* rather than the word *letter* has been that *epistle* has referred to an entire book in the New Testament by Paul, which may have been composed of only one letter or several. *Letter*, on the other hand, has referred to one unit of correspondence, a single "piece of mail."

This, however, is not the only distinction that has ever been made between the two terms. Around the turn of this century, when Egypt was yielding up papyrus letters in great abundance and scholars first began to look to them for light on early Christian literature, one of the greatest to do

The Difference It Makes

so was a German named Adolf Deissmann. He wanted to distinguish between "real" letters, letters that were intended to be sent as correspondence, and "non-real" ones, documents disguised as letters. The real letters he called "letters" and the non-real ones he called "epistles." His distinction has been well stated by Stanley Sowers.

Letters are private, unliterary, purely occasional, and artless and merely convey information, like a telephone call today. Epistles are exemplified by the literary letters—not real letters at all—of writers such as Epicurus, Seneca, and Pliny; they are public (meant for publication or a wider audience), literary, conventional, and artful and are written for posterity. Letters are warm and personal; epistles are cold and impersonal. (*Letter Writing in Greco-Roman Antiquity*, p. 18)

While the distinction made by Deissmann has been extremely influential, and it does point to a significant reality, scholars now recognize that it is overdrawn. Great care can be taken in writing personal letters. When the correspondence of a famous person is published, readers are often astonished by its eloquence. And the fact that it came to be published does not mean that it was not originally intended as a way of communicating with an individual who was absent. Thus the formality and the good quality of a letter do not keep it from being a real letter. It is helpful for the reader to know of Deissmann's distinction, since there are still books around that use the terms in his way, but his distinction will not govern the use of *letter* and *epistle* in this book.

The Least Certain Instance

A question not addressed often enough is that of why, if a letter was not written by Paul, it seemed worthwhile to someone later to pretend that it was. This question cannot be fobbed off by saying airily that his authority was being sought for the point of view expressed. While that is undoubtedly true, it does not go very far. Who was expected to read the document? The congregation to whom it was addressed? Was it then concerned with a particular local situation? Or was it already understood as holy scripture and thus addressed to the church at large so that it was an essay disguised as a letter rather than a real letter?

A modern scholar has delineated a spectrum of possibilities for what it could mean to say that a letter was "by" Paul. It could mean that he wrote it out himself or that he dictated it to someone else or that he asked someone to write it for him or that someone took it upon themselves to write it on his behalf or that it was written as if he had written it or that a disciple or a follower of his wrote it or that it is a forgery that has no connection with him. Making a plausible case that Paul did not write a certain epistle involves the development of a plausible case about how it came to be written. Such a case has to be located along this spectrum in a situation in which it would make sense for such a document to be produced.

Uncertainty about many of these issues is probably the reason that many scholars still believe that Paul wrote II Thessalonians. They would see it as having been written just a few weeks after I Thessalonians, so soon after it, in fact, that a third of the whole could consist of phrases and even whole sentences from the first letter. Why would Paul write again to the same church in such a short time, covering much the same ground? Because in the meanwhile false teachers had produced a letter that they claimed was from Paul, saying that the second coming, the "day of the Lord," had already occurred (2:1-2). Paul is writing, therefore, to give them his own authentic teaching, to give them a way of discriminating between his real letters and false ones, and to give them advice about the proper way for Christians to live as they await the return of Christ.

Against the view that II Thessalonians can be reasonably understood as a letter written by Paul is the lack of any indication in the letters known to be genuine that the delay of the second coming was causing a crisis of faith in Paul's lifetime. There is evidence, however, that it began to be a problem about a generation later. Second Thessalonians fits the needs of that time very well. It argues that Christ has not returned because a number of things have not yet occurred that must occur before the end.

That day will not come, unless the rebellion comes first, and the man of lawlessness [the Antichrist] is revealed, the son of perdition, who opposes and exalts himself against every so-called god or object of worship, so that he takes his seat in the temple of God, proclaiming himself to be God. (II Thessalonians 2:3)

This sounds like a countdown of the events of the end, giving clear signs that can be checked off to show exactly at what point Christ can be expected to return. Yet the thrust of the argument is exactly the opposite. The practical advice given in the letter urges Christians to stop acting as though the end were at hand. Instead, they are to settle down to the ordinary round of daily life, busying themselves with its occupations. Those who are expectantly awaiting the end at any moment are called idlers and busybodies (3:11), and the author says that anyone who will not work should not be allowed to eat. The effect of all this, then, is not to help people know exactly when the end will come, but is rather to get their minds off of it, letting them settle down for the long haul of history. If this reading is correct, II Thessalonians is not a letter by Paul but was written to help a later generation deal with its crisis of faith over the delay of the second coming. It must have been written by one of his followers to offer the advice it was thought Paul would give to one of his congregations as it faced a new crisis.

So Near and Yet So Far

The two epistles yet to be considered in this chapter—Ephesians and Colossians—are closely related to each other and to the genuine letters of Paul. Over a third of the phrases and sentences of Colossians appear in Ephesians. A distinguished scholar of an earlier generation, Henry J. Cadbury, has asked in regard to Ephesians: "Which is more likely—that an imitator of Paul in the first century composed a writing ninety or ninety-five percent in accord with Paul's style or that Paul himself wrote a letter diverging five or ten percent from his usual style?" While Cadbury answered his own rhetorical question by opting for Pauline authorship, there are weighty reasons why his position will not be followed in the pages ahead.

Since Colossians seems closer to the genuine letters by Paul, it should be looked at first. There are some differences of literary style. Colossians has longer, less tightly constructed sentences than appear in the letters Paul is known to have written. This could be explained away by saying that he was dictating to someone else, who transcribed his words differently. The real differences—the things that would seem utterly out of character for Paul—are theological positions. Paul, for instance, said that, while Christians are buried with Christ in baptism, they will not rise with him until he returns (see Rom. 6:3-4). Yet Colossians says that Christians have already died *and risen* with Christ. Certainly Paul changed his mind on some issues, but this does not seem likely to have been one of them. His opponents in a number of churches based their claim to superiority on their having already been raised from the dead.

The situation in the congregation at Colossae—which sounds like a genuine crisis in this particular congregation—is reasonably clear. False teachers appear to have come in, representing a Jewish Christian point of view that is at odds with what Paul had taught. This not only involves the sort of issues of Torah observance that are found in Galatians—such as dietary regulations, the Jewish calendar, and circumcision—but it also involves speculations about the nature of the universe. Between human beings and God are postulated a hierarchy of heavenly beings, "principalities and powers." Somehow the mediation of these angelic creatures was thought to be necessary in obtaining salvation through Christ. Possibly some mysterious rites were practiced to accomplish this mediation. This sort of belief was common in the assumptions about religion made throughout the Greco-Roman world and thus the opponents at Colossae appear to be Jewish Christians who lingered too long in the religious cafeteria line of their generation.

The author's refutation of these beliefs involves a quotation of an early Christian hymn (1:15-20), which speaks of Christ's involvement in creation, including the creation of these heavenly beings. Even more important, however, is the assertion that by his crucifixion Christ defeated all these powers and, like a victorious general bringing his conquered enemies back to Rome, he has led them as captives in his triumphal procession. So complete is this victory that Christians have already been raised with Christ and have entered the kingdom. This cosmic kind of belief about Christ also allows the author to speak of Christ as the head of the church, while in the genuine letters Paul speaks only of the church as the body of Christ without giving a particular bodily role to the Lord.

These theological differences in a letter that is so close to the letters Paul certainly wrote suggest that the writer was a close follower of Paul who knew his thought intimately. He thus attempted to meet a crisis in his congregation shortly after Paul's death in the way that he thought his apostle would have gone about it.

In spite of its close resemblances to Colossians in many ways, Ephesians is a later work. One of the main pieces of evidence for that conclusion is that Ephesians is not really a letter, but is instead a treatise disguised as a letter. The titles of biblical books are not taken from the books themselves but were given to them by later editors. This may be seen, for instance, in the way that the books of the Hebrew Scriptures have a different sort of name entirely in Hebrew from the familiar English ones. In Hebrew the books are called by their opening words; Genesis, as an example, is called *Bereshith*, "in the beginning." Thus the mere fact that the title of the book is "To the Ephesians" does not mean that it is a letter to the church at Ephesus.

Nor is there any internal evidence that Ephesian Christians were the audience for which the work was originally written. True, it does have addressees indicated in 1:1, but they are designated as "the saints who are also faithful in Christ Jesus," without geographical restriction. Readers of the King James Version may object that in their Bibles this verse includes the words "which are at Ephesus." Modern translations omit these words, often indicating in a footnote that they appear in some late manuscripts but not in the earliest and best. Furthermore, Ephesians lacks any greetings at the end, a common feature of Paul's letters. There is no indication of any particular crisis to which the epistle is a response. Rather, it seems addressed to the world at large. Thus Ephesians is not a letter but an essay disguised as a letter.

Further evidence of the lateness of Ephesians is the attitude toward apostles it displays. The church is described as "built upon the foundation of the apostles and prophets" (2:20), while 3:5 refers to Christ's "holy apostles and prophets." As staunchly as Paul defended his status as an apostle, it would be out of character for him to exalt his rank in this way. Rather, these passages reflect the attitude of a later generation looking back on a golden age. Also in Ephesians the inclusion of the gentiles in the church is a *fait accompli*, no longer the divisive issue it was during Paul's ministry. Beyond that, the author seems to have a collection of Paul's letters (including Colossians) that he regards as authoritative in some way, a collection from which he borrows extensively. For these and other reasons, Ephesians is regarded as coming from a time between A.D. 90 and 100.

The best explanation that can be offered for why Ephesians was written, then, is that a generation or more after Paul died someone in one of his churches wrote a treatise for all of them to show how he believed Paul's thought would have continued to develop had he lived on into that period. Those developments have much in common with both later Christian orthodoxy and the Gnostic movement that was getting started then. Later Christians can be glad that this writer felt called upon to "update" Paul. Even if Paul himself might not have approved of all the changes, down through the ages Ephesians has been one of the most popular books he was thought to have written. The church would be much poorer without these "forgeries" of Pauline letters—II Thessalonians, Colossians, and Ephesians.

THINGS TO THINK ABOUT

1. Is there any intrinsic reason why the Holy Spirit could not have inspired a pseudonymous book?
2. What are laypeople to believe when equally learned scholars disagree over a question like who wrote a particular book?

3. Why is it so bad, from Paul's point of view, to believe that Christians have already risen with Christ?

4. Why would someone wish to disguise an essay as a letter of Paul? (Hint: how many kinds of Christian writing existed in the first century?)

C H A P T E R
S E V E N

Preaching Through Biography

Ancient Biographical Writing

After the letters of Paul, the next Christian writing to appear was the Gospel According to Mark. Finally the various forms of oral tradition about Jesus discussed in chapter 2 were to be combined into an account of Jesus' life that appears to be arranged chronologically. The information is organized into a life story; it becomes an ancient form of what today would be called a biography—although it lacks many of the characteristics that modern biographies have.

To ordinary present-day Christians this turn of events must appear natural and even inevitable. This is not just because they are familiar with the four Gospels in the New Testament and thus know that things turned out that way. It is also because biography itself is accepted without thought as the inevitable way to inform someone about a historical figure. But these modern reflexes of thought obscure the fact that Mark was not only the first to tell the story of Jesus chronologically and in writing, he was the inventor of the literary form that is denoted by the term *gospel*. Apart from other considerations, that alone means that he must be regarded as a literary genius. Furthermore, the mere fact that this literary form was astonishingly well conceived as a vehicle to present the Christian proclamation about Jesus means that he must be regarded as a theologian of great historical importance.

All of this is not to say, of course, that no biography had been written before, or even that none had been written as a tool of religious propaganda. To see what is unique about the Gospels, one must set them in the context of Greco-Roman and Jewish treatments of the life stories of people. In the historical development of the biographical form, obituaries early played an important role, since the death of someone occasioned reflections on the significance of that person's life. Biography, however, is a complex literary form. It is an organization of shorter elements into a coherent story, and these individual components all have their own literary form that governs their development. Thus, as David Aune (on whom much of the next few pages depends) has said, biography is a literary form that plays "host" to a lot of other literary forms—such as, anecdotes, speeches, maxims, and documents.

Ancient biography was different from modern biography in that it was more interested in the public achievement than in the private life of a person. One of the reasons that is so is that character was not regarded then as something that developed but rather as something given, something persistent throughout life. Character was manifested in public acts, and these acts became instructive in the benefits or disadvantages of having a certain type of character.

Because of this exemplary understanding of the purpose of biography, the main distinctions between lives of various people are made on the basis of vocational roles—such as political leaders, emperors (regarded as a distinct type), philosophers, public speakers, and literary artists. It may seem as if religious leaders have been omitted from this list, but the ancient world did not make a division of life into mutually exclusive categories of the sacred and the secular. Instead, the people saw divine activity behind the accomplishments of most great persons. Some, for instance, were regarded as actually having been begotten by divine beings, while others were only thought to be godlike.

As suggested, one of the main purposes of classical biography was to praise or blame the values represented by the subject of the writing. This means that most biography was propaganda for a particular system of belief. In the Greek world this was far more likely to be a philosophical system than a political one. Philosophy at that time was more like religion today than it was like the technical studies of contemporary philosophers; it had to do essentially with inculcating a way of life. This interest in values overrode curiosity about the subject of the biography and, therefore, moral examples were of more concern than either the historical uniqueness of the subject or even historical accuracy. Plutarch's *Parallel Lives* is a familiar example of this sort of biography.

The Hebrew Scriptures do not contain much biography in the sense of "a discrete prose narrative devoted exclusively to the portrayal of the whole life of a particular individual perceived as historical" (David Aune, *The New Testament in Its Literary Environment*, p. 29). Extended passages are centered around particular individuals, as for example, Genesis deals with Abraham, Isaac, Jacob, and Joseph; Exodus deals with Moses; and I and II Samuel deal with Samuel, Saul, and David. But all of these passages are part of a larger story, the story of God's relations with Israel. While some cycle of stories, such as that of Moses or Elijah and Elisha, might have influenced Mark's ideas of how to write a gospel, nothing in the Hebrew Bible furnishes an exact parallel to the gospel literary form. The first pure biographical forms to appear in Jewish literature were written near the time that the Gospels were and show the influence of Greco-Roman biographical ideals. Thus Jewish religious writing did not furnish Mark with a full-scale model of the gospel form.

With this background, it is possible to set Mark in the context of biographical writing of the time. The idea of a chronologically organized narrative of a person's life comes to Mark from the Greco-Roman culture around him. This is not to say that he was well educated in that culture and was, as a consequence, familiar with its literary forms. His style is popular, not to say folk. One of the chores Matthew and Luke had in editing Mark for their own Gospels was cleaning up his literary style—though neither of them could satisfy the most fastidious standards of their day.

Besides making grammatical errors and giving the same information in several different ways ("that evening, at sundown," 1:32), Mark told his story in the folk style of connecting sentences by saying "and then" (whoever it was did whatever was done). Oddly enough, though, as episodic as this narrative style was, he nevertheless plotted his Gospel in a dramatic way that had more in common with the tragedy of that time than with its biography. As has been pointed out, the Gospel writers were not interested in questions that are so much a part of present-day biography—education, appearance, personality, motivation, and development. Much of this disinterest grows out of the emphasis on examples of virtue rather than on individuality. In the light of all these tendencies against it, the climactic plotting of Mark is the more remarkable.

The Writing of Mark

Before anything else can be said about this Gospel, something needs to said about what it means to call it Mark. The document itself is anonymous; there is no internal indication of who wrote it. As early as the second century, it was thought to have been written by John Mark, who had been a companion of Paul and Silas on the so-called First Missionary Journey. The theory was that Mark became associated with Peter and learned his version of the stories about Jesus. One of the main difficulties with that theory is that many of the stories told in this Gospel contain indications that, far from being the memories of an eyewitness, they have been passed down by word of mouth for some time. This means that neither the name nor the circumstance of the author is known. When the name of Mark is used below, therefore, all that will be meant by it is either this earliest Gospel or the unknown Christian who wrote it.

All in all, one of the most remarkable things about Mark is that it got written at all. To begin with, the author and his Christian contemporaries expected Jesus to return and the world to end at any minute (9:1), which would raise questions about any activity, like writing, that was oriented to the future. But even if that had not been the case, a decision to string all of the individual stories about Jesus into a coherent, chronologically arranged narrative was not an obvious one.

It might be thought that, since Mark called what he wrote a "gospel," he wrote a biography of Jesus to spread the good news of salvation through him. This would accord with the purpose of a gospel as stated in John 20:31, which says that the Fourth Gospel was written so that "you may believe that Jesus is the Christ, the Son of God, and that believing you may have life in his name." And this certainly appears to be part of the purpose of Mark, but there seems to be more to it than that.

There are some unusual features to this Gospel that cannot be accounted for by the theory that simple evangelization was the author's only purpose in writing. To begin with, not only is nothing said about the birth and childhood of Jesus, but also there is not even an account of his appearing after his resurrection. For the first fourteen hundred years of the Gospel's existence, all copies of it had to be laboriously written out by hand and, like all handwork, there are minute variations among all these manuscripts. But all the earliest and best of these end Mark at 16:8, where the women leave the empty tomb, overcome by fear. And, if there are no resurrection appearances, certainly there is no report of the ascension. This means that some of the basic reasons Christians believe that Jesus is the Christ are not contained in Mark's Gospel. If the author's main purpose had been to evangelize, it is hard to believe that he would have left these out.

There are a number of other strange traits of Mark that must be taken into account by any effort to understand the book. One of these is the motif of what was called "the Messianic secret" by the turn-of-the-century German scholar who first brought it to scholarly attention. It involves several features of the Gospel that suggest that, far from spreading the good news about himself, Jesus tried to keep it quiet. The first of these features is Jesus' tendency to tell those whom he has healed not to tell anyone what he has done for them. The second has to do with the unclean spirits and demons that Jesus casts out of people. These spirits and demons have supernatural knowledge of the identity of Jesus, but he also forbids them to make him known. The last feature has to do with the one group to whom Jesus does communicate anything about himself, his own closest followers. They seem incapable of understanding him and, indeed, seem progressively alienated from him in the course of the Gospel. At only one time does Jesus admit that he is "the Christ, the Son of the Blessed," and that is to the high priest at his trial—thus himself supplying the evidence that convicts him and leads to his execution.

Another unusual aspect of Mark has to do with titles applied to Jesus. Remarkably, "Christ," which comes from the Greek translation of the Hebrew word for "anointed" (*Mashiach*, transliterated as "Messiah"), is not the most common or significant. Rather, there seem to be two main titles. One is Son of God. This should not be confused with the later term of Christian orthodoxy, "God the Son." While the one term leads to the other, there is considerable development between them. The only way to be sure of what Mark means by the term is to see how he uses it. For him it seems to be the key category for understanding Jesus. It probably appears in Mark 1:1, although some good early manuscripts omit it. The title is certainly implied by the voice from heaven at Jesus' baptism and transfiguration. And it is the verdict on Jesus of the Roman centurion in charge of his crucifixion (15:39). Thus Jesus' messianic identity may have been a secret from the other characters in the Gospel, but it is not a secret from the evangelist, and he lets the reader in on the secret from the very beginning.

The other important title in Mark is "Son of Man." Just as Son of God is not to be understood as a reference to the divine nature of the incarnate Lord, so also Son of Man is not to be understood as a reference to his human nature. In some ways, Son of Man could have been regarded as a title superior to Son of God in the time of Jesus. As noted above, many of the great people about whom Greco-Roman biographies were written were regarded as sons of the gods. Yet Son of Man may have been a title from Jewish thought that referred to a glorious supernatural figure who would come at the end of time to judge human beings. One of the ways the term is used in Mark has that meaning; Mark 13:26 refers to "the Son of Man coming in clouds with great power and glory" (compare Dan. 7:13-14). At other times, though, Son of Man just seems to be a way that Jesus refers to himself, an indirect way of saying "I." Finally, Jesus also uses the term in three predictions of his own suffering, death, and resurrection. (See Mark 8:31, 9:31, and 10:33-34.)

This reference to Jesus' suffering and death points to one of the oddest features of Mark: his emphasis on suffering. At the beginning of this century, a scholar described Mark as "a passion narrative with an extended introduction." It is true that six of Mark's sixteen chapters are devoted to the final week of Jesus' life, which is now known liturgically as

"Holy Week." Further, the final outcome of Jesus' struggle with the religious authorities is signaled quite early on. Mark 3:6 states that "the Pharisees went out, and immediately held counsel with the Herodians against him, how to destroy him." And the three predictions of Jesus' death referred to above give shape to the section that begins with Peter's confession that Jesus is the Christ and ends with the arrival in Jerusalem (8:27–10:45). There is little doubt, then, that the crucifixion casts its shadow over the entire Gospel of Mark.

Yet, there is more to it than that. At the beginning of the Gospel, at any rate, all of the emphasis seems to be on Jesus' success. Jesus seems to go from strength to strength in performing one miracle after another. The veneration in which he was held is expressed in the exclamation of the crowd in 7:37: "He has done all things well; he even makes the deaf hear and the [mute] speak." Earlier the disciples had asked: "Who then is this, that even wind and sea obey him?" (4:41).

When one asks how a career that seemed to start out with such promise should take such a disastrous turn, the answer seems to lie in the response of Jesus' closest followers to what was revealed about him. The disciples' misunderstanding of Jesus, mentioned above, seems to have been responsible. It reaches a climax of a sort just after some of the most stupendous miracles Jesus performed. After having twice seen him feed a multitude from a tiny lunch, the disciples, riding with Jesus across the Lake of Galilee, became very upset that they had neglected to pack a lunch. It seemed that no amount of evidence was adequate to enable them to understand what Jesus was capable of.

Shortly after that he checked their knowledge of his identity. He asked them who they thought he was, and Peter immediately said that he was the Christ. At that point, the first of the three predictions of Jesus' death comes. But when Jesus said that he was going to die, Peter began to try to talk him out of it. This showed how completely Peter had misunderstood. He may have come up with a correct title, but he had no idea of the content of that title, what being Christ would involve for Jesus. Apparently he and the rest of the disciples had a view of messiahship that involved great success, a triumphal procession in which all would be swept before Jesus in the recognition of his miraculous powers. Maybe Mark even intends to show them as understanding messiahship on the model of David, the warrior king who drove out all the enemies of Israel (see 12:35-37).

They were not in the market for a messiah whose vocation involved being "delivered to the chief priests and the scribes . . . [who] will condemn him to death, and deliver him to the Gentiles . . . [who] will mock him, and spit upon him, and scourge him, and kill him" (10:33-34). Nevertheless, shortly after Peter's uncomprehending confession, Jesus stripped away all that veiled his true nature and stood transfigured before them as the glorious Son of Man who will come at the end of time to judge all humanity. Each of the passion predictions is followed by two things: an act by one or more of the disciples showing the extent of their misunderstanding (usually having to do with their own importance) and an act by someone from outside the circle of the disciples that showed real penetration into the spirit of Jesus. It is no accident that Mark sandwiches these three predictions of Jesus' death between two stories of the healing of a blind person because the disciples who could see physically could not see spiritually, while those Jesus healed were physically sightless, but spiritually they were sharp sighted indeed. No wonder that by the end of the journey to Jerusalem, the disciples could not bear to walk beside him on the road (10:32). No wonder that by the time the crucifixion actually occurred, they had all fled.

Mark's way of telling the story of Jesus shows that he must have had purposes in mind in addition to simple proclamation of the good news of salvation in Jesus. All of this emphasis on suffering and the alienation of Jesus' closest followers does not really fit into that triumphant tale. Why, then, did Mark write his Gospel—the first Gospel there was—in the way he did? This, unfortunately, is not a question that scholars have been able to agree upon. Thus what will follow will not be *the* correct answer to this question, but will instead represent several answers that have been proposed, several efforts to account for why Mark wrote his Gospel in the first place and why he wrote it the way he did.

One theory is that the disciples are "the bad guys." Its advocates point to the ambiguity of Mark 16:8, the last verse of the Gospel in the earliest manuscripts, which says that the women who came to the tomb on Easter morning "went out and fled from the tomb; for trembling and astonishment had come upon them; and they said nothing to any one, for they were afraid." According to these scholars, when Mark says that the women said nothing to anyone, he means exactly that; the disciples, who had been progressively estranged from Jesus throughout the Gospel, were not informed by the women of the resurrection, and no resurrection appearances were made to them by Jesus. They had, in effect, defected from the Jesus movement and were no longer its representatives. The explanation offered for why Mark would write a Gospel that took such a stand was that he belonged to an early Christian community that was in conflict with that represented by the Twelve in Jerusalem. This form of the life of Jesus, then, was written by one early Christian group to discredit another.

This theory does have the advantage of paying close attention to the text of Mark and not reading into it ideas that have been gathered from elsewhere. An interesting variation on this theme sees the opponents of Mark's community to be the community that produced Q. It will be remembered from chapter 2 that Q was produced by an early Palestinian community of Christians who believed that the risen Christ continued to speak to them through their prophets. Since *Q* is essentially a collection of the sayings of Jesus (and of the risen Lord through the community's prophets), *Q* does not have a passion narrative and never really deals with Christ's suffering. Perhaps the *Q* community's sense of Easter joy in the continued presence of the risen Christ in their midst, as that was revealed in the ecstatic oracles of their prophets, blinded them to the suffering that was yet required of the followers of the Crucified. The fall of Jerusalem in the Jewish Revolt against Rome in A.D. 66–70 could have been the catalyst that caused Mark to put the Jesus tradition in a written form that would stop the manufacture of new sayings of Jesus. That would account for his writing a story of Jesus that was entirely pre-resurrection, an account that dealt faithfully with his suffering and death. It would also account for the sparsity of teaching material in Mark, where the only two major concentrations are the parable material in chapter 4 and the teaching about the end-time in chapter 13.

A third theory takes its departure from a few indications in Mark that the Gospel may have been written in Rome. These include the use of Latin words in the Greek text, a translation of any Aramaic terms used as well as an explanation of Jewish customs, and Mark's use of a Roman method of reckoning time. Some documents from the end of the second century say that Mark's Gospel comes from Rome. If that tradition is accurate, what was going on in Rome about that time that would have conditioned the writing of the Gospel? Mark is believed to have been written in the late 60s, when Nero attempted to blame Christians for the burning of Rome and persecuted them until he died in A.D. 68. The persecuted Christians in Rome would also be aware of the suffering of Jews in Palestine during the revolt against Rome, sufferings in which any Christians who remained would be caught up. In such a situation, endangered Christians did not need to hear so much the triumphalism of impressive miracle stories as they needed to be called to identify their suffering with the suffering of their Lord. Nothing could have been more relevant and helpful to them in their situation. According to this theory, then, Mark would have decided to write his biography of Jesus to help the members of his Christian community at Rome to make sense of the suffering they were called upon to endure.

THINGS TO THINK ABOUT

1. Were you surprised by the list of things a Gospel might be expected to contain that are missing from Mark? Why?
2. Now that you have heard the theory of the Messianic Secret motif in Mark, is it consistent with your reading of the Gospel? Do the phenomena pointed to actually occur?
3. Which of the theories about why Mark was written makes most sense to you?
4. What place do you think Mark deserves in the history of literature?

C H A P T E R

E I G H T

The Book of the True People of God

How Matthew and Luke Wrote

One of the most useful tools for anyone wishing to study the first three Gospels is called a *synopsis*. It derives from Greek words meaning "things that can be seen together." It takes the form of setting Matthew, Mark, and Luke in parallel columns. For this reason, such books are also called *parallels*. When the three versions of the gospel are set side by side, a number of things are made obvious.

* Each one has some material that none of the others has.
* Almost everything in Mark appears also in Matthew and Luke.
* At times the wording is so nearly identical as to make it likely that two copied from the third or all three copied from the same other document.
* Matthew and Luke share extensive material that does not appear in Mark, which is often so similar in wording that it suggests copying.

The effort to account for these similarities and differences occasions what scholars call "the synoptic problem." For some time most scholars have accepted as a solution to the synoptic problem some variation of what is called either the "two-source" or the "four-source" theory. By this is meant that when Matthew and Luke sat down to write their

Gospels, they had two documents open in front of them from which they copied extensively and which they edited to suit their purposes. These are the Gospel of Mark and the collection of sayings material that is called the Q document. As may be inferred from this, scholars believe that Matthew and Luke copied from Mark, rather than from each other or from some outside source, and that they did depend on an outside source for the material they have in common that is not shared with Mark.

Thus it is assumed that Matthew and Luke shared two of the same sources: Mark and Q. At the same time, it is obvious that each had access to material the other did not. For instance, the stories about Jesus' birth in Matthew are very different from those in Luke. Matthew concentrates on Joseph, while Luke is more interested in Mary. The "wise men" appear only in Matthew, and the shepherds are mentioned in Luke alone. The list could be lengthened, but enough has been said to make it clear that in the infancy stories as in a number of other places, Matthew and Luke are not drawing from the same sources. To refer to the material that is exclusive to Matthew alone or Luke alone, scholars use the terms M and L. The use of these terms does not mean that these two Gospel writers each had only one source additional to Mark and Q. No, it is assumed that each had received material from a number of different sources—and that each created material as it was needed. M and L, then, are just convenient terms to refer to anything in Matthew that is not in Luke and vice versa. Together with Mark and Q, then, M and L make up the four sources of the four-source theory.

This information furnishes real insight into the process by which Matthew and Luke wrote their Gospels. They wove together a number of strands of material. In the main, they merged large blocks of Mark and Q, but in addition they blended in other material. Since, in spite of having so much material in common, the two complete Gospels are very different from one another, it seems clear that their author/editors had different goals in mind when they sat down to compose. Since we have no contemporary information other than the Gospels themselves—not even the names of the writers; these Gospels are as anonymous as Mark—then all that can be known about what those goals were has to be inferred from their finished products, the Gospels themselves as they have come down to us.

Observing Matthew

Much can be learned about Matthew just by a careful examination of what is in it. It is obvious that Matthew's basic framework comes from Mark; 90 percent of Mark appears in Matthew. Since Mark is arranged chronologically, it is not surprising that Matthew follows Mark's basic sequence—although not without variation. Yet, there are large blocks of material at the beginning and end of Matthew that have no equivalent in Mark. The infancy stories mentioned above are on one end and, since Mark ends at 16:8 with no one seeing the risen Lord, Matthew's resurrection appearance scenes are on the other.

But that is not all. Matthew also incorporates much teaching material that is absent from Mark. The portion of that which is shared with Luke is, of course, Q. Matthew has a very different way of fitting that material into his Gospel from the one followed by Luke. Matthew interrupts his Markan sequence at five points to insert blocks of teaching material that thus seem like continuous speeches made on the occasions in the narrative in which they appear. Thus chapters 5 to 7 are the beloved "Sermon on the Mount," 9:36–10:42 is a final word of advice to the Twelve as they are sent on their mission, chapter 13 is Matthew's concentration of parables and teaching about them, chapter 18 deals with discipline within the Christian community, and chapters 23 to 25 are about the final judgment. Each of these sections ends with the same words: "Now when Jesus had finished these sayings. . . ."

It is an oversimplification to say that these five blocks of teaching material are from *Q*. Much of Matthew's *Q* material does appear in these speeches, but that is not all that is in them. Mark's parable and apocalyptic materials from chapters 4 and 13, for instance, are used by Matthew in his discourses on those topics, and Mark's shorter instruction to the disciples departing on their mission is drawn on for Matthew's version of the same talk. Furthermore, these five speeches also incorporate material that is not shared with either Mark or Luke; sections of *M* are drawn on. Thus the speeches as they appear are not just the mechanical repetition of something that appeared elsewhere in the same form. Rather, they represent careful editorial activity by Matthew in blending material drawn from a number of sources so that each sounds like a unified treatment of a subject that belongs together. And, since it was Matthew who gave the material that unity and shape, it was assembled to serve some editorial purpose he had.

One clue to what these purposes might have been is the nature of *M* material. Whatever the means by which it came to Matthew, he chose to include it and thus presumably it accomplishes something he wanted done. Several blocks of it have already been referred to, such as the infancy stories (prefaced with Jesus' genealogy) and accounts of appearances of the risen Lord. Mention has also been made of *M* material in the five long speeches. There are also additions to Mark's narrative—such as the reluctance of John the Baptist to baptize Jesus, the coin in the fish's mouth, the suicide of Judas, the dream of Pilate's wife and Pilate's hand washing, and the resurrection of the saints at the time of the crucifixion.

Probably the most distinctive *M* material, though, is a collection of about a dozen proof texts from the Hebrew

Scriptures that is scattered through the Gospel, although five of them appear in the first two chapters among the infancy stories. These texts are introduced with a formula like "all this took place to fulfill what the Lord had spoken by the prophet." While much of the theology of the New Testament is framed in terms of such an understanding of the Hebrew Bible as containing veiled prophecies of Christ, the number of these "testimonies" in Matthew and the form they take have led some scholars to formulate a theory about how this Gospel came to be written. As noted in an earlier chapter, this sort of biblical interpretation was also done at Qumran by the community that produced the Dead Sea Scrolls. It also has much in common with biblical interpretation done by early rabbis. This theory, then, is that Matthew was produced for a community of Jewish Christians that had its own rabbis who devoted their time to combing the scriptures for what they understood as prophecies of Christ.

A Christian Community in Controversy

This inventory of the arrangement of Matthew and of the material that is exclusive to this Gospel makes it possible to begin to say something about why it was written. A great medieval theologian argued for the existence of God by saying that the material universe is an effect that implies a cause. That is to say that the universe does not account for its own existence and so it must have some outside cause that can account for it. Then he asked what sort of cause that would be. His answer was that it was a cause capable of producing such an effect. It takes an artist to produce a work of art, and it takes a boilermaker to make a boiler. It takes a congress to create a law for this nation (as recognized by the comedian who said: "Laws are made incongruous"). This is to say that you can learn a lot about the creators of anything by looking at what they created. This principle applies to the writers of Gospels as well as to the creators of boilers, works of art, and universes. What, then, can we learn about "Matthew" from the Gospel that bears his name?

To begin with, he thought the whole life of Jesus was important, not just his ministry and crucifixion. He was interested in Jesus' birth and his resurrection, and he was also interested in what Jesus taught. His efforts to see predictions of Jesus in the Hebrew Scriptures implies that he was a part of a community that regarded those scriptures as inspired, whose understanding of Jesus was based on them, which suggests that the community was predominantly Jewish.

This Jewish character is further brought out by a number of passages in which Jesus' interpretation of the Torah is placed against that of the Pharisees. The Pharisees were one of the reform movements within Judaism with which the Jesus movement was most in competition. That conflict carried on into Matthew's time when Pharisaism was almost the only one of the reform movements left. But just as the Jesus movement was becoming the Christian church, so also Pharisaism was becoming the Judaism of the rabbis, the Judaism that was to be "normative"—to use one scholar's term—until the Enlightenment of the eighteenth century. This Pharisaic/rabbinic tradition understood the Torah essentially as instruction in the way that the people of God were expected to live. Most of the instructions had to do with issues of ceremonial purity. These passages in Matthew reflect controversies between his community and the Judaism of his time that are argued in terms of how Jesus disagreed with the Pharisees who were contemporary with him.

All of this is much too abstract, but it can be easily understood when examples are examined. These can be found in abundance near the beginning of the Sermon on the Mount. Jesus' relations to the Torah are stated in 5:17-18.

Think not that I have come to abolish the law [Torah] and the prophets [the second division of the Hebrew canon]; I have come not to abolish them but to fulfil them. For truly, I say to you, till heaven and earth pass away, not an iota, not a dot, will pass from the law until all is accomplished.

The point is reached in 5:20: "For I tell you, unless your righteousness exceeds that of the scribes and Pharisees, you will never enter the kingdom of heaven."

The issue, then, is the difference between the Pharisees' interpretation of the Torah and that of Jesus. After this introduction comes a series of examples introduced by some formula, such as: "You have heard that it was said to the men of old. . . ." These examples have to do with what could be called the "spiritualization" of the commandments against murder, adultery, and false witness. These are followed by discussions of revenge and attitudes toward enemies, which move on to standards for religious duties such as almsgiving, prayer, and fasting. All of these discussions contrast the righteousness expected of Christians, the righteousness that exceeds that of the Torah scholars (scribes) and Pharisees, with that of Matthew's opponents.

Three passages in Matthew sum up in one way or another the principle behind Jesus' interpretation of the Torah. One occurs at the climax of the Sermon on the Mount. It is the familiar "Golden Rule": "Whatever you wish that men would do to you, do so to them; for that is the law and the prophets" (7:12). As a matter of fact, what Jesus said here is not so different from the teaching of the Pharisees. One of their great teachers, Hillel, was once asked to summarize the Torah while standing on one foot—that is, in a very short time. His reply has been called "the negative Golden Rule": "Whatever is hateful to you, do not do to your neighbor. That is the entire Torah. The rest is commentary; go and learn it." The difference between Jesus and Hillel seems to be that Jesus thought that his key to the interpretation of the Torah took precedence over any specific provision of the Torah, a position that Pharisees would not allow. Thus Jesus was continually disputing with them over whether healing and other such activities should be performed on the Sabbath.

The second statement of Jesus' principle for interpreting the Torah is the well-known "summary of the law," found in 22:37-40:

You shall love the Lord your God with all your heart, and with all your soul, and with all your mind. This is the great and first commandment. And a second is like it, You shall love your neighbor as yourself. On these two commandments depend all the law and the prophets.

For Jesus, then, the key to all law is the law of love. This becomes very clear in the parable of the judgment in chapter 25. The basis on which the sheep are separated from the goats, the righteous from the unrighteous, the saved from the damned, is whether they have fed the hungry, given drink to the thirsty, welcomed the stranger, clothed the naked, visited the sick, and gone to those in prison.

If, then, a major concern is to oppose the interpretation of the Torah of Jesus and the early Christians to that of the Pharisees and early rabbis, this sheds some light on the construction of Matthew. It has been noted that in between Matthew's birth narratives and his account of Jesus' death and resurrection the material is divided into five narrative sections, each of which is followed by a long block of Jesus' teaching. Since the Torah is composed of five books, maybe this fivefold division of Matthew is to be reminiscent of the

Torah. It would not, of course, be "the New Torah," because Jesus has said that the old will not pass away even in its smallest detail. Instead, the entire Gospel represents the Christian key to the Torah that is set in contrast to Pharisaic principles of interpretation.

By now it must be pretty obvious that the Pharisees—or their successors contemporary with Matthew, the rabbis—were deeply involved in the reason for the writing of Matthew. That raises the question of what they were doing that should have prompted such a response. The answer has already been suggested in an earlier chapter. After the Jewish-Roman war, the rabbis retired to the coastal town of Jamnia, or Jabneh, to consolidate what remained of the religious community and to see what could be done about carrying on their religion after the destruction of the Temple. By this time it had already become recognized that Christianity posed a great threat to Judaism and that Judaism would have to distinguish itself from Christianity and dissociate the two communities if it were to survive in a form acceptable to the rabbis. Thus a number of actions were taken to ensure the separation of what were now to be regarded as two distinct religions. The chief of these was the formulation of the canon of Hebrew Scriptures, and the second was to incorporate into one of the principal prayers of the synagogue service, the Eighteen Benedictions, a curse on Christians. The effect of these two actions was to drive Christians out of the Jewish religious community.

Seen in this light, the purpose of Matthew becomes clear: it is to justify Christianity's right to be considered not only as a legitimate party within Israel but also as its only authentic representative. Matthew, in its response to the actions of Jabneh, becomes a sort of Christian declaration of independence, which says that the Christian church is the true Israel, the only people of God. Thus Matthew has written an apologia, a justification, for the Christian community. That explains why Matthew is the only Gospel to use the word *church*. He uses it in 16:18, where Jesus says that upon the rock of Peter he will build his church, and again in 18:17 in the discussion of what to do about a Christian who persists in sin after many warnings.

Matthew, then, was written to "excommunicate" the Pharisees and their heirs, the rabbis. They do not represent the true people of God because the Christian church does. This is a Christian response to being ejected from the religious community by the rabbis at Jabneh. This understanding of Matthew is borne out by what many would regard as the most unpromising part of Matthew for any sort of theological depth, the genealogy with which the Gospel begins. Although many Christians with good intentions to read the Bible "straight through from 'kiver' to 'kiver'" have shipwrecked on the rocks of the "begats" that occur early in the first book of each of the testaments, one can nevertheless, like Samson, find honey in the dry bones (see Judg. 14:8).

To begin with, Jesus' descent is traced back to Abraham, the father of the religious community. Then the key to the genealogy is given in 1:17: "So all the generations from Abraham to David were fourteen generations, and from David to the deportation to Babylon fourteen generations, and from the deportation to Babylon to the Christ were fourteen generations." This schematized summary, which has to bend some of the biblical data to work out so neatly, points to refoundings of the religious community. Started originally with Abraham, it got a new beginning under David, the first great king. It is to be noted that Jesus is called "son of David" as well as "son of Abraham" in 1:1. Then the community was refounded after the Babylonian captivity as no longer an independent nation under its own king but as a religious community incorporated into someone else's empire. Since Jesus comes at the end of the next fourteen generations, it is obvious that the new refounding has been done through him.

The refounding of the community by Jesus is not just to be on a par with the other major transitions. Rather, Jesus is to stand alone as preeminent over all his predecessors, as different in kind from them. This is proved by the infancy narratives and, as David L. Barr has cogently argued, this is the real issue of the first ten chapters (see David L. Barr, *New Testament Story: An Introduction* [Belmont, Calif.: Wadsworth, 1987], pp. 177-82). Matthew, then, appears to us as the response of a Jewish Christian congregation to the expulsion of Christians from the synagogue by the rabbis at Jabneh. Its author and his community had the gravest possible need to respond by viewing the followers of Jesus in a different light.

THINGS TO THINK ABOUT

1. If you do not have one, borrow a Gospel parallel or synopsis from a library or your pastor and examine it. How does it support the four-source theory?

2. What is your reaction to the suggestion that the Gospel writers copied from written sources?

3. Much of the theology of the New Testament consists of seeing predictions of Christ in the Hebrew Scriptures. Do you think the writers of those scriptures knew that they were prophesying about Christ? Does their attitude make any difference in how seriously you take the interpretation of their writings that is made in the New Testament? Explain.

4. What do you think of the claim made, in effect, by Matthew that Christianity rather than rabbinic Judaism is the true heir of the religion of Israel?

The Most Beautiful Book in the World

The Beloved Physician?

There is little doubt which book would be chosen if a poll were taken to discover the all-time favorite book in the Bible for Christians. The Gospel According to Luke would win hands down. There are a number of reasons this is so. One is that the favorite book would almost have to be a Gospel because Christians love to hear the story of their Lord. Mark would not be chosen because it does not have the wonderful teaching material from Q that is in Matthew and Luke. John's main claim to favor is the same as its chief drawback: it sounds so ethereal. So the contest is between Matthew and Luke. But Matthew is so occupied with issues of interpretation of the Torah that it seems remote from us.

Luke, on the other hand, has so much going for it. To begin with, from a literary point of view it is one of the best written books in the New Testament, being second only to the Epistle to the Hebrews. Luke and its companion volume, Acts, appear to be the only writings in the New Testament that were intended for pagan as well as Christian readers. One theory has it that the prefaces with which the two of them start indicate that the books were intended for the general book market. Included in the superiority of the writing in Luke is the author's capacity to create unforgettable scenes of drama and inspiration.

But more is at stake than literary skill. There is something about the content. Luke, for instance, is so often the evangelist who calls attention to the neglected, less privileged members of society—the poor, the Samaritans, and women. He shows Jesus as the compassionate one. This comes out in favorite parables that appear nowhere else, such as that of the good Samaritan and the prodigal son. It is Luke who gives us beloved canticles we use in worship, such as the songs of Mary *(Magnificat)* and Simeon *(Nunc dimittis)*. It is he who tells of the annunciation to Mary, the birth of John the Baptist, and the visit of the shepherds. And it is he who reports on the supper at Emmaus, in which the risen Lord is made known to two of his disciples in the breaking of the bread. Furthermore, Luke has more to say about prayer and about the Holy Spirit than any of the other Gospel writers.

The qualities shown by its author in this Gospel have caused Christians of all generations to wonder who Luke was. But he no more tells his identity than any other evangelist. He names the person to whom he dedicates his two books; he calls him Theophilus—which means a lover or friend of God—but he does not give his own name. This, however, has not prevented pious guesses. Most of them have centered around the fact that there are a number of places in Acts (16:10-17; 20:5-15; 21:1-18; and 27:1–28:16) in which the author moves from the third person to the first person and stops speaking of what "they" did and begins to talk of what "we" did. This makes it sound as though the author of Acts—and therefore of Luke—was someone who had been with Paul at those times.

As a result, curious Christians pored over the lists of companions that occur in letters attributed to Paul. They found one candidate who seemed to have been with him at the appropriate times. In Philemon 23-24, one of the companions of Paul who is listed as joining in Paul's greetings is someone called Luke. A Luke is also named in a similar list in Colossians 4:10-14; there he is referred to as "the beloved physician." Finally, in II Timothy 4:11, after telling how he has been deserted by everyone else, Paul is depicted as making the deeply moving assertion that "only Luke is with me."

How nicely it all fit together! One who had devoted his life to the healing arts would be the one who emphasized the compassion of Jesus. The faithful companion of Paul who had stuck with him when no one else did would be the one responsible for our knowledge of Paul's missionary activities. This reconstruction was completed by the second half of the second century and has convinced most Bible scholars before the modern era and continues to convince a large number today.

Problems arose, however, when it began to be noticed that two of the references to Luke, those that refer to him as a physician and as Paul's sole remaining companion, are in books that are not thought to have been written by Paul: Colossians and II Timothy. That would not be too devastating, since the reference in Philemon is genuine. The real puzzler, though, is that in all its account of the missionary activity of Paul, Acts makes no mention of the thing for which he is best known to contemporary Christians: the letters he wrote. Not only that, the teaching that Paul does in Acts does not deal with the same issues as Paul discusses in his letters, and in many ways the theological perspective seems diametrically opposed to that of Paul. Could someone who was Paul's constant companion have misunderstood him so thoroughly?

Their conviction that such a companion could not have been so uncomprehending has led a large number of modern scholars to say that Luke and Acts were not written by the Luke mentioned in the Pauline letters. Instead, they say, the works represent the perspective of a third-generation Christian, one who looks back on the time of Acts as the Golden Age.

Other scholars who recognize these difficulties, however, are not convinced that they necessarily mean that a companion of Paul could not have written Luke and Acts. They point out that this two-volume work must have been written relatively late, since it reflects knowledge of the Jewish-Roman war of A.D. 66–70 and also comes from a time when Mark, which was written just before or after A.D. 70, was so widely circulated that an author could use it for a source. On the other hand it could not have been written too late since it must have come out before Paul's letters had been collected and circulated as a unit. This means that Luke and Acts were probably written sometime between 85 and 95. And, since the date of Paul's death is not known, it can be said that Luke-Acts was written somewhere between twenty and forty years after the death of Paul. After so long a time, the issues that were of concern to Paul would no longer be those that occupied the attention of the church. But the author would have been writing to address issues that were current at the time. Thus a real eyewitness and companion could have produced this portrait that is so unrecognizable to those who know Paul from his letters.

What is the upshot of all this? Did the beloved physician write Luke-Acts? The questions cannot be positively decided one way or the other, but those who prefer to believe he did must remember that doing so does not guarantee the accuracy of all that he says about Paul. It disagrees too much at points with what Paul himself said. But that will come up in the next chapter when Acts is discussed.

Luke's Story of Jesus

The way to begin to discover what Luke (that is, the one who wrote the two volumes, without making any presupposition about what else he may have done) was trying to accomplish by writing his Gospel the way he did is to look at how he used his sources. The four-source theory has it that Luke had Mark and Q before him when he wrote and that he also incorporated into his work a variety of other material—no doubt coming from a number of places, including his own creative imagination—that is lumped together under the designation of L.

Since changing L to M would be all that was needed to make this the list of Matthew's sources, it is really surprising that two works that have so much common material could be so different. The difference between them is in their special sources and, even more, in the way that they used their various sources. While Matthew divided Q (and some of his special material) into five long discourses that he inserted into the narrative of Mark, Luke used most of Q in a series of talks that Jesus gave on the journey from Galilee to Jerusalem. This journey, which takes only a chapter in Mark, has been expanded to occupy the middle third of Luke (9:51–19:28). Since most of what has been inserted is teaching material from Q, the journey seems not so much like a trip with a destination as like an aimlessly ambling teaching tour that happens to wind up at Jerusalem.

As with Matthew, a good bit of Luke's special material is concentrated in his stories of Jesus' infancy and his death and resurrection. As indicated above, the infancy stories are told from the point of view of Mary rather than Joseph and tell of the visit of the shepherds rather than the wise men. Another feature of this material is that many of the stories of the birth of Jesus are paralleled with others about the birth of John the Baptist. Also included in this L material is the only Gospel record of an event in Jesus' childhood: his visit to the Temple at the age of twelve. While there are many differences of detail between the passion narratives of Luke and Matthew, one of the most important is that Jesus' resurrection appearance to the disciples occurs in Jerusalem in Luke, while Matthew sets it in Galilee. It is obvious that Luke's purpose in having it occur in Jerusalem is to provide continuity with all the events that will be narrated in the Acts of the Apostles. Indeed, a common feature of the way Luke edited his Gospel is his way of connecting the story of Jesus with the story of the early church, which he tells in his second volume.

An Important Theory

Until recently, the efforts of New Testament scholars to interpret what Luke was trying to accomplish by his use of his sources were dominated by the work of German scholar Hans Conzelmann. His study of Luke-Acts, translated into English in 1961 under the title of *The Theology of St. Luke*, had an original German title that meant "the middle of time." That title indicates a key to Conzelmann's interpretation of the Lukan writings. He believed that Luke thought of time as being divided into three periods: (1) the time of Israel (the salvation history of Hebrew Scriptures, which lasted through the ministry of John the Baptist); (2) the time of salvation (the life of Jesus, especially the time between his temptation and Judas' decision to betray him); and (3) the time of the church (from Pentecost to the time of writing—that is, the period covered by Acts).

Thus the middle of time was the time of salvation during the ministry of Jesus. What made that time the time of salvation was the inactivity of Satan. At the end of the account of Jesus' temptation, Luke says in 4:13 that Satan left Jesus "until an opportune time." Then he does not mention Satan again until 22:3, when he says that Satan entered into Judas Iscariot. Conzelmann understands Luke to be saying that the time between those two events was a time when Satan was inactive, which made it a foretaste of the kingdom of God.

Conzelmann saw this division of time into three periods as part of an elaborate argument Luke was making to deal with a crisis of faith in the church of his time over the delay of Christ's return. The first Christians expected this second coming (referred to in Greek as Jesus' *parousia*, his presence or appearance) to come at any minute. But some fifty or sixty years later when Luke was writing, Conzelmann argues, this hope had begun to dim. People cannot stand forever on "the tiptoe of expectation" (Luke 3:15 NEB). They began to doubt that Jesus was coming soon and thus began to question the church, which had promised that he would. Luke wrote his two-volume work, therefore, to show that God had never intended for Christ to return so early; God had always intended for there to be a significant period between the ascension and the parousia.

According to Conzelmann, proving that God had intended this significant period was what motivated Luke to follow up his story of Jesus with a history of the early church. By showing in Acts that the delay of Jesus' return had permitted the mission to the gentiles and the transfer of the church's center from Jerusalem to Rome and that this expansion of the church had been directed at every turn by the Holy Spirit and had been predicted in the Hebrew Scriptures, Luke was able to show that God had meant all along for a considerable period of time to elapse between the ascension and the second coming.

The Plan of Salvation

As impressive as Conzelmann's achievement is, recent scholarship as a whole has reacted against it. While many of his findings will be permanent acquisitions of insight, very few students of the Gospels today accept his interpretation as a whole. Many have noted, for instance, that his thesis that John the Baptist belongs to the time of Israel and that Luke uses a number of devices to separate John's mission from the activity of Jesus depends on treating the infancy stories as not a part of Luke's design. Most scholars consider these stories to be so obviously Lukan that they cannot accept that stipulation. Under such pressures, the rigid separation of time into three eras begins to collapse.

And, for myself at any rate, there is no necessity for such a division of time, because there is no evidence that there was a crisis of faith at the time over the delay of the second coming. Thus Conzelmann's interpretation of Luke's solution is unnecessary when what he understood to be Luke's problem appears not to have existed.

Saying this, however, completely reopens the question of Luke's purpose in writing. Some of the positive accomplishments of Conzelmann's work give a good foundation for building anew. His discernment that in Acts the mission to the gentiles and movement of the center of the church from Jerusalem to Rome was both motivated at every turn by the Holy Spirit and prophesied in the Hebrew Scriptures calls attention to a feature of the two-volume work that is of primary importance: the way that everything that happens is seen to have been prophesied. While Luke does not use the sort of formula citations or proof texts that Matthew does, his work is no less an argument from prophecy.

This can be seen, for instance, in the way that most of the speeches in Acts have the same outline. They say that something was prophesied in the Hebrew Scriptures, that it was fulfilled in the life of Jesus, that the apostles are witnesses to this fulfillment, and that the audience should therefore repent and accept the Gospel. Conzelmann saw the basic purpose of Jesus' ministry in Galilee as being the assembly of this group of witnesses so that during the rest of his ministry they could be observing the fulfillments that they would later report.

It can be seen even more clearly in Jesus' sermon in his hometown of Nazareth. Luke alone indicates the content of that sermon. It is based on Isaiah 61:1-2 and 58:6.

> The Spirit of the Lord is upon me,
> because he has anointed me to
>   preach good news to the poor.
> He has sent me to proclaim release
>   to the captives
> and recovering of sight to the blind,
> to set at liberty those who are
>   oppressed,
> to proclaim the acceptable year of
>   the Lord.
> (Luke 4:18)

Jesus interpreted this passage to be a prophecy of himself: "Today this scripture has been fulfilled in your hearing" (Luke 4:21).

The close correlation between the things predicted in this passage from Isaiah and the activities in which Jesus engaged shows that the sermon stated the programme of his ministry.

The same point is made when John the Baptist sent to Jesus from prison to find out if he were the One who was to come. Jesus does not answer the question directly, but tells the messengers to report to John what Jesus was doing. The list of activities matches the things predicted of the Messiah in the text from Isaiah, on which he preached at Nazareth, and other texts like it (7:22). When the messengers have left,

Jesus speaks of the identity of John in terms of another passage from prophecy, Malachi 3:1, thus identifying John as the herald of the Messiah.

The key passage for understanding Luke's doctrine of Christ is not in his Gospel but in Acts 5:23, where Peter quotes Deuteronomy 18:15-16 to the effect that Jesus is the prophet like Moses, who was promised in that passage. By this is meant not just a later figure who would be equal to Moses, but the superior figure who would fulfill all the promises of the Hebrew Scriptures and who would bring the salvation that Moses gave only by way of symbolic promise. Thus everything that Jesus did had been prophesied. Further, he was a prophet himself, telling what would happen to him and what would come after him. Finally, as noted above, the prophecies of old predicted not only Jesus but also the activities of the early church and such activities in world history as the fall of Jerusalem.

All of this makes it possible to offer an interpretation of Luke's purpose in writing. It has been seen that Matthew interpreted passages from the Hebrew Scriptures as part of a controversy his Christian synagogue was having with Pharisees over the correct understanding of Torah. Luke, however, was addressing fellow gentiles who did not accept the inspiration of Hebrew Scriptures. Thus his use of the argument from prophecy had to be different. It had to say, in effect, that prophecies that come true are true prophecies. Whatever they predict, therefore, has to have the significance they say it has. Thus it becomes a circular argument proving Jesus from the Scriptures and the Scriptures from Jesus. But it has a validity because both things exist: the prophecies and their fulfillment. Furthermore, the prophecies are brought right down to the situation of Luke's audience. It is shown in Acts how the promise of old to Israel is made available to them right then in the missionary work of the church. All they have to do is repent and believe in order to inherit all of the good things that God had planned originally and that the Holy Spirit had caused the prophets to predict. The totally reliable plan of salvation is being offered to them right then. Luke's purpose in writing his two-volume work was to extend the missionary work begun by Paul and the apostles and to make its offer of salvation to gentile readers of Luke's day.

THINGS TO THINK ABOUT

1. What is your favorite book in the New Testament? Why?
2. Who do you think wrote Luke-Acts? Why? Would it disturb you if you were proved wrong in this?
3. Do you find the "atmosphere" of Luke different from that of Matthew? In what ways?
4. Is the sort of interpretation done by Conzelmann stimulating to you? Is it helpful to your understanding?
5. How would you distinguish between Matthew's argument from prophecy and that of Luke?

CHAPTER

TEN

Apostolic Adventures

What Kind of Book Is This?

Even though a good bit has been said about Acts already in the discussion of its companion volume, Luke, recent study has cast enough new light on Luke's story of the early church to make it worth looking at in its own right and in some detail. It is unique among the writings of the New Testament as the only account of the expansion of the Christian community after the ascension. While the letters of Paul and other epistles reflect this process, none of them furnish a narrative account of it. In the days when it was assumed that Acts had been written by a companion of Paul, it could be further presupposed that the book consisted in part of the reminiscences of an eyewitness and in part of what had been told to him by people who had participated in the events at which he was not present. In recent times, however, when it has become apparent that the portrait that Acts gives of Paul is in many ways inconsistent with what Paul reveals about himself in his own letters, this confidence in Acts as an eyewitness account has been weakened. Thus the question of the kind of book Acts is has been reopened.

One way of approaching the issues involved in the current discussion is to take one chapter and see what kind of writing it represents. Chapter 19 furnishes an excellent case study because it deals with Paul's longest stay in one city. In fact, it is better to begin a few verses earlier to get background information for understanding chapter 19. Chapter 18 tells of how Paul had preached in Corinth and had met there and become associated with Aquila and Priscilla, fellow leather workers who had been driven out of Rome by the Emperor Claudius. Paul lived and worked with them while he established the church in that city. Then he took them with him as far as Ephesus on his return trip to Jerusalem. While at Ephesus he preached in the synagogue once, and the Ephesian Jews asked him to return, which he promised to do.

Chapter eighteen, verses 24-28, deals with a Christian leader named Apollos, who had begun to evangelize Ephesus. He was from Alexandria, Egypt, a great center of Judaism and, indeed, the intellectual capital of the ancient world. It was there that Jewish scholars like Philo applied to the Hebrew Scriptures the allegorical method of interpretation that Greek philosophers used with the works of Homer. Apollos is described as "well versed in the Scriptures," which sounds appropriate for a Jew from Alexandria. He was already a convert to Christianity and had begun to preach in the synagogue in Ephesus and give a Christian interpretation of the lessons read there from the Torah and the prophets. But his knowledge of Christianity was incomplete; he knew John's baptism of repentance but not Jesus' baptism in the Holy Spirit. Luckily, however, the newly arrived Priscilla and Aquila (the wife is often mentioned first, which may mean that she was the more important Christian worker) were able to set him straight. After that, he felt called to preach in Corinth, and the Christian community in Ephesus sent him there with appropriate letters of commendation.

Chapter 19 thus begins with Paul's promise to return to Ephesus. There he found a Christian community already in existence, although they had not yet profited from the correction of Aquila and Priscilla as Apollos had, so they still had received only John's baptism of repentance and had not even heard of the existence of the Holy Spirit. When they heard of the blessings still in store for them, they were anxious to receive them, so they were baptized. Paul laid hands on them in completion of their rite of initiation into the Spirit-filled community. That the initiation was complete was immediately apparent because the Ephesians began to engage in ecstatic utterance (which Luke uses in Acts to document a valid extension of the Christian community).

At first there were only about twelve members of the Christian community in Ephesus, but Paul went right to work preaching in the synagogue. He did so for only about three months before there was a split between those who accepted his contention that Christianity was the true religion of Israel and those who did not. Forming a synagogue of their own, the Christians began to meet daily in a rented lecture hall, and Paul's eloquence was so great that by the end of two years the Christian message had been heard not only by all of the residents of the city but even by all those who lived in the province of Asia (the western third of modern Turkey) as well.

And Paul was as impressive in deed as in word. Not only did he heal many sick people directly, but cloths that had touched him were used to cure many others as well. So impressive, in fact, was his ability to heal that his methods were copied by the local miracle workers who were so much a part of the scene in the Greco-Roman world. Among these were the sons of a Jewish high priest (whose name is not in any historical records). When, however, they said to an evil spirit, "I adjure you by the Jesus whom Paul preaches," the spirit responded by saying, "Jesus I know and Paul I know, but who are you?" and drove them outside beaten up with their clothes torn off them. This so impressed the local populace that the magicians, for whom the city was famous in antiquity, gave up their craft and even burned their books of spells—books that had a market value of more than fifteen years' wages for a working man.

Paul then decided to complete that tour and began to make arrangements for his departure, but other events were brewing. Ephesus was the location of one of the Seven Wonders of the ancient world, the magnificent temple of a goddess—known by the Greek and Roman names of Artemis and Diana—who appears to have been more like the mother goddess of an oriental fertility cult, such as Cybele or Atargatis. The temple was a pilgrim shrine, and local merchants derived a good bit of their income from selling religious objects to those who came to worship. Silversmiths especially did well by manufacturing small silver replicas of the shrine. But Paul's success had been so great that business had fallen off sharply for both the shrine and the artisans.

Stirred up by one of their number named Demetrius, the silversmiths began to riot and dragged two of Paul's companions with them into the huge open-air theater there in order to have a public assembly deal with the issue. Paul wanted to speak to the crowd and rescue his assistants, but he was dissuaded not only by his followers but even by—so great had his fame and popularity become—the elected religious leaders of the province of Asia *who had the responsibility for promoting the worship of the Roman emperor as a god.* When it looked like the whole occasion was going to turn into a pogrom of the Jews, one of the two main officials of the city assured the crowd that the Christians were not a threat to their goddess and that such rioting could provoke sanctions from the Roman government. Chapter 20 begins by giving the information that as soon as all this was quieted down Paul went ahead with his plans to leave.

How thrilling all of this is! What a great demonstration of the power of the gospel! Paul begins with a group of a dozen ill-instructed Christians and in less than three years he could leave behind a church whose message had been heard by everyone in an enormous province. It was a church in which miracles could be performed regularly through relics of Paul to the envy of all the professional miracle workers, one that had its good name defended by the civil administration of the city and even had seen the safety of its apostle become a major concern with the pagan religious leaders of the entire province.

When all of this has been said, however, one can begin to notice what has been omitted in this breathtaking narrative. First of all it can be seen that only four concrete events are mentioned for the entire period. Then it can be said that nothing is reported about the growth of the community. There is no mention of who the first converts were, who the leaders in the congregation were, how this wonderful work of evangelism throughout the province was accomplished, how the community was organized, what its worship was like, or many other things that devout curiosity would love to learn. Think of it this way: If the congregation of First Church, Ephesus, wanted to have its history written to celebrate a significant anniversary, as many local churches do today, almost none of the information that one would expect such a history to contain is conveyed to us in this account of its founding.

When that becomes clear, it can then be observed that the account is not really a record of the beginning of the congregation in Ephesus but is instead an account of some of Paul's activities in Ephesus. The chapter deals with the actions of an individual rather than the history of a community. Paul is the hero of the story; the interest is all focused on him. Not only that, but the interest is all focused on certain kinds of his activities. Nothing is said about his evangelistic methods or even about the content of his teaching beyond his distinction between the baptism of John the Baptist and that of Jesus.

Nor is anything said about what can be gleaned from the letters of Paul about his activities in Ephesus. For instance, most scholars think that Paul wrote Galatians, much of the Corinthian correspondence, Philippians, and Philemon from Ephesus. Why is nothing said anywhere in the entire book of Acts about this correspondence, or indeed about any of the letters we have from Paul? And these letters were written from prison. Paul never says in so many words that he was imprisoned in Ephesus, but he does mention being imprisoned often (II Cor. 11:23) and that he "fought with the beasts at Ephesus" (I Cor. 15:32). If Paul were in prison there, why is nothing said about that?

What is given instead of all these things that could have been included in this chapter is a report of exciting events—the thrilling experience of the conferral of the Holy Spirit; the briefly noted break with the synagogue, which led to the rental of a hall and Paul's astonishing success as a speaker; the rather humorous account of how some religious charlatans got their comeuppance; and a mob scene in which the civil and pagan religious leaders of the community came to the defense of Christians against the threat of important businessmen in the city.

Lest it be thought that the nineteenth chapter is exceptional, it can be pointed out that it represents instead what is par for the course. A study of the type of literature to which Acts belongs has been made recently by Richard Pervo in his book *Profit with Delight*. His analysis of the events reported in Acts breaks them down into six categories: (1) imprisonments; (2) persecutions and martyrdoms; (3) plots, conspiracies, and intrigues; (4) crowds, mobs, riots, and assemblies; (5) trials, legal action, and punishment; and (6) shipwreck and travel. He also categorizes other material in Acts as dealing with (1) humor and wit, as seen in irony (as when the exorcists in Ephesus were trounced by the demon); (2) burlesque and rowdy episodes (like Paul's cure of a woman possessed by a prophetic spirit in chapter 16); (3) cleverness and wit (as in the story of the boy who fell asleep when Paul was preaching in chapter 20); (4) pathos (the raising of Tabitha, chapter 9); (5) utopian, exotic, and colorful scenes (the "primitive communism" of Acts 2 and 4); (6) exotica and orientalia (the Ethiopian eunuch in chapter 8); (7) oratory and letter writing (speeches constitute a third of the content of Acts); and (8) life in high society (Paul's friendship with the Asiarchs in Ephesus). It is to be noted that the examples enclosed in parentheses are not the only ones that could be given but are simply an indication of the kind of content that is referred to by the category.

The significance of Pervo's analysis is the light it sheds on Luke's purpose in writing Acts. Apparently Luke did not expect his readers to be very interested in the sort of institutional history that would be regarded as a Godsend by Christians today who are eager to learn how their religion got started. He sees them instead as the sort of people who like an exciting story. That probably makes them like most people today. Technical studies by historians can count on only a small sale among other professional scholars and the libraries that cater to them; such books are very expensive to publish, since sales are so light. Good historical works written for the general public will range from selling several thousand copies to the rare success of books, like those by Barbara Tuchmann, that make the bestseller list. Not even these "blockbusters," however, have the audience of millions like that of a television mini-series that brings a historical era or event to life in the form of a suspenseful drama. Most of us prefer reading exciting adventure stories to studying historical scholarship.

Historical Reliability

The issue here is not how accurate the historical record in Acts is. It has much more to do with the kinds of things that

Luke decided to tell—and not to tell. Modern standards of verifiability in historical writing were unknown to the ancient world, and nothing written as history in classical times would be accepted as totally reliable by any historian of today.

It has already been stated that some of what Acts has to say about Paul cannot be relied upon because it is inconsistent with what Paul himself said (chapter 3). This has to do not only with the sequence of events or exactly what happened where, but also what Paul taught. It has been noted already that most of the speeches in Acts have the same outline. This means, for instance, that Paul preaches essentially what Peter does. But Galatians 2:11-21 (where Peter is referred to as Cephas) suggests real differences between the two apostles. The difference between the teaching of the real Paul and that of Paul as depicted in Acts has been delineated most sharply by Philipp Vielhauer in an article published in the early 1950s. He shows sharp disagreements between the two on basic issues like natural theology, the status of the Torah, the doctrine of Christ, and belief about last things. Most scholars would probably say that Vielhauer exaggerated these differences, but few would say they do not exist.

The point of all this is not to say that Luke intended to mislead anyone by writing Acts. Nor is it even to suggest that Acts is terribly different from other books in the Bible. Jesus taught by parables, and his teaching was no less true because the events he related never occurred. Scholars agree that at least one book in the Bible, Jonah, is a parable—out and out fiction, but no less true or religiously important for that. Esther sounds like fiction, as do Judith, Tobit, Susanna, Bel and the Dragon, and other books in the Apocrypha. The book of Daniel was not written in the time of the Babylonian captivity in which it is set, but is a work of underground propaganda produced during the period just before the revolt of Judas Maccabeus. Nor were all of the oracles in the books of the prophets spoken by the prophet in whose book they occur, as the distinction between First, Second, and Third Isaiah indicates. And it has already been noted that some of the epistles attributed to Paul were not written by him. It will be noted later on that the letters attributed to Peter, James, and Jude were not written by them. Thus there is some sense in which none of these pseudonymous writings is literally and historically true.

Yet, that finding does not suggest that they should be removed from the canon or that they were not inspired by the Holy Spirit or that Christians should have less confidence in their ability to mediate God's Word to them for the direction of their lives and the formation of their faith. It is hard for contemporary people whose consciousness has been shaped so much by the concept of scientific historiography to believe, but literal historical truth is not the only, or even the most important, sort of truth there is. God's ways of self-revelation are much more subtle and nuanced than that.

Which is to say that the value Christians place on the Acts of the Apostles is not directly proportional to its historical reliability. At the same time, however, it must be insisted that Acts is by no means devoid of reliable historical information about the early church; it contains much. But like a good historical novel, that is not all that it contains. It also contains the efforts of the marvelous literary ability of Luke to bring the story alive so that his contemporaries would be excited about it, persuaded by it, and converted to Christianity.

Acts fails to relay much information that contemporary Christians would give their eye teeth to get. It tells only of Paul's mission among the gentiles and thus does not say anything about how the faith spread to places where he did not found the church, such as Rome or Alexandria. It does not even tell everything about Paul's work that devout curiosity wishes to know. One of the most influential works on missionary strategy today is a book by Roland Allen called *Missionary Method: St. Paul's or Ours?* If Acts had conveyed even more information about how Paul had actually worked, how useful that would have been to a church that needs so badly to evangelize and even to re-evangelize.

Yet, it is ungrateful to complain that one of the least forgettable books ever written does not do things that it never intended to do. One should rather take it and enjoy it for the wonderful and inspiring story of faith that it is.

THINGS TO THINK ABOUT

1. Does the sensational nature of the material in Acts seem to you to be inconsistent with the character of historical writing? Why?

2. Does the religious truth of a biblical book depend on its historical accuracy?

3. Is your faith in biblical inspiration weakened by this chapter, or is it deepened and widened? Explain.

4. Is it consistent with the nature of Holy Scripture that a biblical book be fun to read?

The Tradition of the Beloved Disciple

A Spiritual Gospel

Clement, a Christian writer from Alexandria who lived A.D. 150–215, tried to put in writing what he had come to believe about the order in which the Gospels were written. Far from agreeing with modern scholars that Mark was written first, he stated that the two with genealogies (Matthew and Luke) had that honor. Then he went on to say: "Last of all, aware that the physical facts had been recorded in the Gospels, encouraged by his pupils and irresistibly moved by the Spirit, John wrote a spiritual gospel" (quoted in Eusebius, *History of the Church* 6.14.7).

Any modern Christian who is at all familiar with the New Testament knows what is meant by calling John a "spiritual" Gospel, although one might have difficulty putting it into precise words. Part of what is meant is that the Gospel starts off differently, with that wonderfully poetic sounding prologue that begins: "In the beginning was the Word and the Word was with God and the Word was God." But more is meant than this. There's something that goes through the entire Gospel that makes Jesus sound different from the way he sounds in the other Gospels. Modern scholars may have gone too far when they said something like "the Jesus of the Fourth Gospel sounds like he walks around with his feet eighteen inches off the ground" or "he doesn't eat or drink like other people," but we know what they were getting at. John's Jesus is closer than the Jesus portrayed in the Synoptics to the Jesus of a certain kind of religious movie in which he is always dressed in white, has his head backlighted by the sun in a halo effect, and has organ music on the soundtrack whenever he speaks. It's all very ethereal.

This description may make it sound a little funny and as though what is talked about were a shortcoming, but that is not the way it is. This spiritual quality is really rather beautiful, and most Christians would feel impoverished indeed if they were to lose this Gospel.

What is the "spiritual" quality at stake here? Can it be specified a little more clearly? What is there about the Gospel According to John that causes people to react to it the way they do? These questions can probably be best approached by a simple catalog of basic differences between John and the Synoptics. It can be started with noting that the locale of the ministry of Jesus is not the same. In all the synoptic Gospels, the only time before Holy Week that Jesus leaves the northern area of Palestine to go to the area around Jerusalem is his pilgrim visit to the Temple when he is twelve, which is recorded by Luke. In the Fourth Gospel, however, Jesus takes his disciples to Jerusalem for feasts on numerous occasions. Indeed, his public ministry begins there at a Passover celebration, when he cleanses the Temple, something that he does not do before Holy Week in the other Gospels.

This reference to feasts at Jerusalem suggests what is also true—that the time of Jesus' ministry, as well as its place, is more extensive in John. The only incident in Mark that really requires Jesus' ministry to have lasted longer than one year is the incident of his disciples' plucking off grains when they walked through a wheat field (2:23 ff.). Since harvest time in Palestine is in the spring and since Jesus was crucified in the spring and the wheat plucking seems not to have occurred in the same spring as the crucifixion, Jesus' ministry must have lasted at least a little over a year. In John, though, the chronology is very different. At least three and maybe four of the feasts for which Jesus goes to Jerusalem are Passovers. Since Passover occurs only once a year, then Jesus' ministry in John is seen as having lasted several years.

Then, too, the order of events is not always the same. It has already been noted that in John the cleansing of the Temple came at the beginning, rather than the end, of Jesus' ministry. In the Synoptics, the cleansing is the catalyst that sets events in motion that will result in the crucifixion. That function is served in John by the raising from the dead of Jesus' friend Lazarus, an event and person not even mentioned in the other Gospels. There are a number of stories in John that have no parallel in the Synoptics: the wedding at Cana, the story of how Nicodemus came to Jesus by night, and the story of the woman at the well, to mention but a few. John also gives a number of details, especially about places in Jerusalem, that (a) are reported nowhere else and (b) have been verified by archaeology.

By the same token, John leaves out a number of things that the other Gospels relate. For instance, he does not directly tell of Jesus' baptism and does not mention the institution of the eucharist at the Last Supper—although at other places the sacraments appear to be taken for granted by the author. Also missing are events that show Jesus in stress, such as his temptation or the agony in the garden of Gethsemane. Even the crucifixion does not seem like the incredibly painful event that it was, but is instead Jesus' "lift off" for his return to the heavenly world from which he came. Jesus' teaching by parables, such an important aspect of the synoptic portrait of him, is absent, replaced by a different sort of figure of speech. Nor is anything said about his casting out unclean spirits; the only references to being possessed by demons make that a synonym for insanity, and the charge is directed against Jesus. Indeed, fewer of Jesus' miracles are reported, but somehow those that are seem more miraculous. They are even called by the special word "signs."

Furthermore, the way that Jesus speaks is very different in John. While the Synoptics report several long sermons that he preached (such as the five discourses into which most of the Q material of Matthew is divided), seldom do they seem like real speeches with introduction, body, and conclusion, with an argument developed in the body. As a matter of fact, each verse often seems like a complete thought in itself, what comedians would call "one liners," were they not so serious. In John, though, the speeches are developed discourses. Even when Jesus starts off in a dialogue with someone else, soon he alone is speaking and doing so, not in a conversational flitting from topic to topic, but in a well-organized presentation of thought. Often, though, one can notice that a statement similar to one of the "one liners" from the synoptics will be the point that a discourse in John is making, the thesis of the speech.

Not only is the way Jesus speaks his message different in John, but what he has to say is also different. In the Synoptics the subject of Jesus' preaching is the kingdom of God (or of heaven in Matthew, in compliance with the Jewish reverence for the name of God). Yet the kingdom is mentioned only once in John (3:3). The nearest equivalent of the effect of Jesus' ministry is "eternal life," which is a very different concept in that it focuses not on the changed situation in the universe brought about by the restoration of God's rule over history but on the personal result for individuals of accepting Jesus' proclamation.

A study of the way that Jesus speaks of life (with or without the adjective *eternal)* calls attention to another difference in his teaching as recorded by John. Life is often contrasted with death as the alternatives that are posed to human beings. Not only that, this is only one of a number of contrasted pairs: light/darkness, truth/falsehood, above/below, of this world/not of this world. Furthermore, these contrasted pairs seem to be interchangeable. Each seems to refer to the ultimate choice that people have to make in life. And this choice boils down to accepting Jesus and his message or not doing so. These interchangeable contrasted pairs are one of the features of John that makes it seem like such a "spiritual Gospel."

The Word Made Flesh

The vocabulary of Jesus' preaching in John suggests that this Gospel represents a thought world different from that of the Synoptics. If the dynamic of this system can be delineated, it might be possible to identify the environment in which it developed and thus to move on and say something about how this remarkable Gospel came to be written and also something about other literature in the New Testament that is closely related to it.

John has left one sentence that furnishes a very concise summary of all that he has to say. That sentence is such a familiar and beloved compression of the entire Christian faith that it is a favorite Bible verse of many. Indeed, anyone who watches athletic events on television is likely to see it cited on a banner that always manages to get in camera range. This verse, of course, is John 3:16: "For God so loved the world that he gave his only Son, that whoever believes in him should not perish but have eternal life."

Perhaps the best term to begin with is *world*. While it can refer to the physical universe, in this case "the world" means humanity. It was human beings whom God loved. In other places in John *world* can mean humanity in a negative sense, humanity organized against God. Here, though, it represents God's concern for the entire human race. Thus it was not just Israel whom Jesus came to save, but gentiles as well.

Incidentally, the Gospel was written in a non-Jewish environment; the author, therefore, does not break down the resistance to Jesus of the religious establishment into such groups as Sadducees or scribes and Pharisees. Rather, they are lumped together as "the Jews." Thus they represent a special case of the world as humanity organized against God. This cannot be anti-Semitism in the modern sense at all because it is probable that all the early leaders in the Johannine community were Jewish. Rather, it reflects the time when Christians were excluded from the synagogues (9:22; 12:42; 16:2). This was probably before the general exclusion after Jabneh and had to do with particular beliefs of the Johannine Christians (see below).

The King James Version translates "only Son" as "only begotten Son." In general, the RSV is correct in rendering the Greek word involved as "only" or "unique," but King James should be preferred here because (a) a root relating to birth is a component of the Greek word *(monogenes)*, and (b) the Fourth Gospel has an understanding of Christ as the Begotten Son of God that is unique in the New Testament. This is part of what it means to say: "He was in the beginning with God; all things were made through him, and without him was not anything made that was made" (1:2-3). In modern theological language, this is to say that Christ was the Father's agent of creation, who thus existed before the universe and even shared the Father's divinity. John combines two ways of speaking about Christ, one that speaks of him as subordinate to the Father and another that does not hesitate to call him God. This ambiguity is never resolved; two apparently inconsistent truths continue to be maintained. It was not until the church councils of the fourth century that all of the logical implications of this were worked out in the doctrines of Christ's divine and human natures and of the one God as being the Trinity of Father, Son, and Holy Spirit.

This insight applied to John 3:16 explains how a contemporary Roman Catholic artist, Corita Kent, could apply to Christ the advertising slogan of a greeting card company: "When you care enough to send the very best." God's compassion for humanity was so great that God's own self took on the human condition to reconcile all humanity to God's self.

The contrasts spoken of above may be seen here. The alternatives presented in this verse are perishing or having eternal life. The basic metaphor of salvation that is used here, then, is not the apocalyptic temporal metaphor of the two ages that is seen in the Synoptics. The effect of Christ is not spoken of as bringing to an end the present evil age under the domination of the powers of evil and inaugurating the age to come, in which God's rule over history has been restored. Rather, it is the spatial metaphor of the Divine Word coming down from the eternal realm of God above to the transitory human world below in order to make it possible for human beings to return with Christ to the eternal realm above. Since life down here ends in death because this world passes away, the only way that human beings can live forever is to be taken into the world above. Thus "above" equals "life" and "below" equals "perishing" or "death." For that reason, the realm above is also "true" and "real," while this world is "false" and "unreal." Thus the eternal Word of God became "flesh," became fully human in order that human beings may have eternal life with God.

What determines whether human beings inherit eternal life or perish has nothing to do with any inherent value of their own. John does not have a Gnostic conviction that those to be saved are flecks of the divine nature that somehow became imprisoned in flesh and need only to learn of their heavenly origin in order to be released. No, what determines who will be saved and who will be lost is a choice that each person will have to make, a choice between believing in Christ or not believing in him. It all boils down to accepting Jesus' claim that he is the One whom the Father has sent to show his love.

The Community of the Johannine Literature

Enough has now been said to make it possible to account for the differences between the Johannine and the synoptic reports of the life and teaching of Jesus. This explanation will be based on the reconstruction of the historical situation made by Raymond E. Brown in his book *The Community of the Beloved Disciple*. It begins by noting that the accurate historical details found in John but not elsewhere show that this Gospel was not made up out of whole cloth but goes back to memories of eyewitnesses for its earliest material. One of those eyewitnesses seems to have been the figure referred to in the Gospel as "the beloved Disciple" and similar terms (21:24), although that person does not appear to have been the apostle John, the son of Zebedee, with whom he has traditionally been identified. Although this disciple may have been the disciple of John the Baptist rather than Andrew, who followed Jesus in 1:35 ff., he is not explicitly spoken of until the last supper. Thus he does not appear to have been one of the Twelve who went around with Jesus during his ministry. In fact, the frequent comparisons of his behavior to Peter's (in which Peter never comes out ahead) suggests some rivalry between the Johannine community and that which centered around the Twelve.

Thus this Gospel would represent a tradition about Jesus that would be as early and as reliable as that in the Synoptics. The time that the community that received that tradition began to look different from the one around the

Twelve, however, goes back to around A.D. 50 when this group amalgamated with a group of Jewish followers of Jesus who had converted some Samaritans. This group had a bias against the Temple and thus were more interested in a Messiah like Moses than one like David, one who had brought God's Word to his people. The mixture of these two communities caused the development of an understanding of Christ that was much more in the direction that Christian orthodoxy was going to develop than the synoptic tradition. Its Samaritan and Mosaic emphases led it to recognize that the Savior would have to be preexistent and divine. These beliefs about Jesus were very threatening to the Jewish community, who thought they were inconsistent with the unity of God. Thus they began to expel the Johannine Christians from their synagogues.

The response of the ousted and rejected Christians was twofold. On the one hand, they could only interpret the ones who had ejected them as being motivated by evil rather than good; therefore, they came to see "the Jews" as the extreme example of "the world," as humanity organized against God. On the other hand, they consoled themselves over their loss by concentrating on their salvation as something they already enjoyed. Thus they lost much of their interest in the second coming and began to think of eternal life not as something begun after death but as something entered upon whenever one came to believe the Christian faith. The time between these Johannine Christians becoming identifiable as a distinct Christian community and the writing of the Fourth Gospel probably extended from around A.D. 50 to around A.D. 90.

The writing reflected a kind of meditation on both the actions of Jesus (the "signs") and his teaching (the "discourses") that had been going on for some time, a sort of reflection that came to understand what Jesus had said and done in the perspective of their own theological emphases. This accounts for the different tone of the Fourth

Gospel and shows how individual sayings of Jesus familiar from the Synoptics could have been expanded into the developed speeches of John.

It was probably around this time that the inhospitality of Palestine prompted the Johannine community to recognize a call to a mission to the gentiles and to move to some center in the Greco-Roman world, perhaps Ephesus with which tradition associates the Fourth Gospel. In this move, the community began both to develop its own universalistic views that Christ was the Savior of the whole world and to recognize that gentiles were not necessarily more open to the gospel than the unbelieving Jews had been. It became clearer that humanity, "the world," resists God.

Up until this time, the community had been united. The threats it had perceived had been from external groups— such as the world at large, "the Jews" (in the sense of those who had ejected them from the synagogue), and followers of John the Baptist, who considered him rather than Jesus to be the Messiah. The Gospel also shows traces of opposition to Jewish Christians afraid to admit their identity, lapsed Christians, and, to an extent, the community around the Twelve.

Now, however, a split arose within the Johannine community. Its emphasis on the preexistence and divinity of Christ permitted some members to question the reality of his humanity. They appeared to deny that he had "come in the flesh." Thus they did not see the importance of the earthly life of Jesus as an example for their own. They developed such a confidence in their own salvation that ethical behavior, even "loving one another," ceased to appear necessary to them. Thus sometime around A.D. 100 they separated themselves from the community.

Someone who remained within the community set out to demonstrate their errors. It was obvious that their belief came from a distortion of the doctrine of Christ in the Fourth Gospel. Someone who had been in the community for a long time and knew how the tradition had developed and knew the correctives to this overemphasis on Christ's divinity that lay in the early memories of the life of Jesus wrote the First Letter of John to point out the errors of the dissidents. Second and Third John represent efforts to deal with error within the community through church organization that gives control of teaching into the hands of leaders.

The writing of the Johannine epistles does not seem to have been successful in luring the secessionists back into the community. Thus in a relatively short time the Johannine community as a separate Christian tradition passed out of existence. Those who had remained in the community began to see the need for closer association with the mainstream of the church, represented in the community that had built up around the Twelve. By this time, that tradition was much more open to the high doctrine of Christ that the Johannine community had taught and there was no real reason for the two streams of tradition to stay apart. Meanwhile, the secessionists, who must have comprised the larger part of the Johannine community, began to explore theological directions that would eventually lead into such heresies as Docetism (denying the reality of Christ's humanity), Gnosticism, and Montanism (an overdevelopment of the Johannine doctrine of the Holy Spirit [Paraclete] that led "prophets" to claim that they embodied the Spirit).

One modern scholar has called John the "maverick" Gospel and, as is shown by the break-up of its community into dissenting groups—some of which became heretical—some risk is involved in including it in the canon. Its spirituality needs to be balanced by the emphasis of the Synoptics on Jesus' earthly life. At the same time, John's emphasis on Christ and the Spirit are an important corrective on any tendency of the Synoptics to get too down to earth, matter of fact, and institutional. Thus the two streams of tradition are mutually corrective and make it possible for the church today to enjoy the fullness of faith that it has.

THINGS TO THINK ABOUT

1. Which do you like better, John or the Synoptics? Why?
2. How would you characterize the differences between Jesus as he appears in John and in the Synoptics?
3. Does John's picture of Christ as the Father's preexistent agent of creation seem to you the logical implication of the understanding the Synoptics have of Jesus' significance?
4. Does it seem natural to you that the Johannine community should have had such a split as that reflected in I John? Why?

C H A P T E R

T W E L V E

The Long Haul
of History

An Institution in Society

By the end of the first Christian century, much had happened to the movement that Jesus had begun as a wandering charismatic prophet in Galilee during the short period of his ministry just before A.D. 30. The movement had spread throughout most of the civilized world of that day. The New Testament has references to its movement north of Palestine into Syria and then west across what today is Turkey to Greece and Italy with Paul's mentioning plans to go to Spain. The discovery of Christian papyri in Egypt, dating to the early second century, including a few verses of John that are dated around 125, suggests that the church may have arrived there before 100. References to Cyrene in Acts, as well as in the Gospels, suggests that there could have been Christians in what is now Libya. And early legends that suggest that one of the apostles evangelized the east cannot be dismissed entirely; certainly a very Jewish kind of Christianity existed from an early date in Edessa in the bend of the Euphrates.

Neither does the diversity of the early church seem to be confined to its geographical diffusion. The discussion of oral tradition in chapter 2 indicated that in the earliest years after the resurrection there were different kinds of Christian communities in Galilee, Jerusalem, and Antioch. While Luke tries to give a picture in Acts of an orderly expansion of the Spirit-filled community that was coordinated by the church at Jerusalem, he is not always able to suppress evidence that there was more variety than that. Paul's letters certainly do not support the contention that he was under orders from Jerusalem. The reconstruction of the history of the Johannine community in the previous chapter also adds to the impression of variegation. And this has not even been to mention the opposition that much New Testament literature indicates early Christian leaders had.

The rapid expansion of Christianity and the proliferation of its varieties, together with the passage of time, which suggested that the world might not end as soon as expected, had two very important implications for the community: (1) the church was becoming an institution in society, and (2) the variety of manifestations of the movement made it difficult to agree upon who represented true Christianity. Thus the church had to think through the implications of its own existence and become much more self-conscious about its institutional life.

This process of institutional self-definition has been referred to by a number of different terms, such as "radical Hellenization" or "early catholicism" by church historians who yearned nostalgically for the charismatic spontaneity of an earlier period. Yet it is hard to see how much alternative there really was. For the religion to expand at all, it had to become an institution. Human life in society is always institutional except in small primary communities where all members have interpersonal relation and decisions can be made informally and ad hoc. The issue for any movement that grows is not whether it will become an institution but what kind of institution it will become.

This process of institutionalization required the identification of norms that could be appealed to in cases of doubt. Essentially four were recognized by what became "main-line" Christianity, "the great church." The first had already been resorted to in Judaism, the making of an approved list of inspired writings that could be appealed to in settling disputed questions. This, then, is the establishment of a Christian canon of Holy Scripture. It would involve the recognition of some Christian writings as having inspiration on a par with that of the Hebrew Scriptures; this is to say that it would involve the canonization of the New Testament.

Then, since this canon would be so voluminous, it would be necessary to have a much more concise statement of Christian belief that would serve as a ready-to-hand criterion by which doctrinal statements could be evaluated. In time this need would be met by the creeds of the church, especially by the so-called Apostles' and Nicene creeds. Earlier on, though, shorter formulas were adopted that could be referred to by such terms as "the pattern of sound words," "the faith once delivered to the saints," and, a good bit later, "the rule of faith."

Standards, though, always need someone to interpret them, so in time there had to be persons who had the official responsibility for both teaching themselves and evaluating the teaching of others. With their offices often went other responsibilities, such as guaranteeing that baptism and the Eucharist would be properly celebrated. Thus it became necessary for offices to develop, for orders of ministry to be conferred. Finally, as has been suggested already, inclusion in or exclusion from the sacraments of initiation and communion could also function as a safeguard of the identity of the Christian body. The process by which the early church began to develop its canon of scriptures, its standards of belief, its authoritative officers, and its sacraments can be studied in New Testament books to be examined in this chapter.

Un-Pauline Paulinists

Since 1726, when they were so designated by Professor Paul Anton of the University of Halle, I and II Timothy and Titus have been called the Pastoral Epistles. A later scholar said that the title stuck because these are writings by a pastor for pastors. This is to suggest that they offer, in effect, a seminary course in pastoral theology. More recent scholars have sharpened this description by identifying the types of literature to which these epistles belong. First Timothy and Titus are seen to resemble each other more than either resembles II Timothy. Each of them is a set of directions about how to organize a Christian community. Written as though they were letters by Paul to two of his assistants to whom he has given the responsibility of organizing the churches in Ephesus and Crete, I Timothy and Titus tell what sort of persons should occupy such offices in the church as bishop/elder, deacon, and widow. There are also instructions for the behavior of other categories of members in the congregations.

A little reflection will identify the literary pattern of these documents. They are an adaptation of the tables of duties for members of a household seen in other epistles attributed to Paul, tables that represent a standard form of moral instruction used at the time by pagan philosophers. Yet, they are not all that helpful as manuals of church administration, nor are they terribly useful to modern scholars interested in the organization of the early church because the main information they give about any of the offices is the moral qualifications for holding them. Further, there is little difference in the qualifications for the various offices or, for that matter, between these Christian lists and those given by pagans for the offices of general, physician, or even actor. The qualifications are the sort of basic, sound middle-class morals that have been approved by every religion for every society.

There is, however, one important exception to the rule that moral qualifications for the offices are discussed rather than duties of the office: duties as well as explicit restrictions are discussed for widows while they are never discussed for male officers, not even bishops. Elisabeth Schuessler Fiorenza is undoubtedly correct in seeing here an attempt to reverse the conditions that prevailed under Paul, in which Priscilla could be a more important leader than her husband and Phoebe's ministry was worth supporting by a letter of commendation (Rom. 16:1-5). She also sees in the description of the office of widow a suggestion that at the time the Pastorals were written, women were already living in religious communities, anticipating the orders of nuns that would begin to be formed in the fourth century (*In Memory of Her*, pp. 309-13; the "her" referred to in the title is the woman referred to in Mark 14:9).

If the literary form of I Timothy and Titus is that of a church organization manual developed from a list of the duties of members of a household, the form of II Timothy is another that is familiar from the Bible and intertestamental literature: it is a "testament." *Testament* here has the sense that it does in "last will and testament" and refers to a literary genre of what claim to be the last words of sainted persons. These offer for those who are to follow instructions on how to carry on in the way that the dying hero would wish. A well-known apocryphal document is called The Testament of the Twelve Patriarchs and, as will emerge later in this chapter, II Peter belong to this genre. Satisfaction of the requirements of this form gives the personal touches to II Timothy that caused an earlier generation to offer the unlikely hypothesis that the Pastorals contain fragments of genuine letters of Paul. It is hard to believe, though, that anyone would throw away the teaching section of real letters from Paul and keep only the personal messages from them.

In several ways it has already been suggested that these epistles were not written by Paul. Although dispute is possible, arguments against Pauline authorship can be advanced on grounds of literary style, vocabulary, theology, historical situation, and church organization. The Pastorals come from a time when the church felt threatened by heretical teachers, and they act as handbooks to leaders on how to recognize those who were going to cause trouble. These tactics are entirely different from those of Paul. He showed what was wrong with the theological positions of his opponents while the Pastor is just content to rule them out of court by calling them heretics. An earlier scholar has said that Paul was inspired, but the Pastor was only orthodox. He must have lived at a time when orthodoxy and order were needed; still one can regret that the price paid for it was sometimes so high.

Open Letters

Reference was made in chapter 6 to Deissmann's distinction between letters and epistles, "real" and "unreal" mail. His distinction was rejected because it was seen that actual correspondence can be quite literary. The distinction can be valid, though, even if Deissmann's characterization of the two categories is rejected. A writing can be given the literary form of a letter that was never intended to be an effort of one human being to communicate with one or more others from whom the author is separated. One way to test whether a writing is genuine correspondence is to apply to it the criterion of deliverability. Would it be possible to deliver that document?

A case in point is the Letter of James. It is addressed to "the twelve tribes of the Dispersion." Literally that means all of the Jews outside of Palestine. Assuming that the Epistle of James is a Christian writing—which all scholars are not willing to do—and thus that the addressees are not the seventh of the population of the Roman Empire made up of Jews but only that portion of them who had accepted the Messiahship of Jesus, the difficulties of the task of delivery would still be insuperable.

Or again, I Peter is addressed to "the [Christian] exiles of the Dispersion in Pontus, Galatia, Cappadocia, Asia, and Bithynia." Here the addressees are not scattered throughout the entire Greco-Roman world, but are confined to Asia Minor. Nevertheless, a map of that area in New Testament times, the sort that is published in the back of many Bibles, will show that Bithynia and Pontus extend over two-thirds of the northern coast of modern Turkey; Asia takes in the western coast, Galatia the central area, and Cappadocia the eastern interior. The southern coastline is all of that vast area that is excluded. Even if the author meant for his writing to be delivered to congregations rather than individuals, a large number of copies would be required. Or if, as is sometimes suggested, the work was a circular letter meant to be carried from place to place by a messenger, the messenger would be gone for a long time.

The addressees of II Peter and Jude are indicated even more vaguely. Thus these writings are referred to either as the "General" Epistles (in the sense of being for everyone) or as the "Catholic" epistles (in the sense of universal)—which is to say that they are not letters at all, but essays disguised as letters.

That fact alone says something about the likelihood that they were written by the persons they claim to be written by. The only reason for giving a treatise epistolary form would have been that this was the authoritative form of early Christian literature. With the exceptions of Acts and the Revelation, every writing in the New Testament has the form of either a Gospel or a letter. The letter form, of course, was inaugurated by Paul as he tried to deal with problems in his congregations when he was absent from them. Thus his letters were real ones and written for practical purposes.

This means that any authority the letter form had came from Paul's use of it. Thus one could not count on that authority until Paul's use of the form was well known, which certainly means after Paul's death and possibly means after his letters came to be circulated as a collection. Yet, James and Peter are known to have died within a relatively short time of Paul, and nothing we know about them suggests that they would have wanted to increase their authority by imitating Paul. Thus the General Epistles seem likely to be pseudonymous.

This does not mean, however, that the names of the letters are insignificant. The choice of the pseudonyms used says a lot about the community of the writer, or at least that of the recipients. It says that these would be people with whom the name of the purported writer carried great weight. Just as the so-called deutero-Pauline epistles (II Thessalonians, Colossians, and Ephesians) and the Pastoral epistles indicate the lingering magic of the name of Paul, so also the catholic epistles show that there continued to be communities in the early Christian world in which the names of the brothers of Jesus and the leader of the Twelve continued to evoke a strong response.

One would expect such communities to have a Jewish Christian character. In Acts, for instance, James is seen as the leader of the church in Jerusalem after Peter left and as one open to the concerns of those who were loyal to the Torah (21:17-26). Such an impression of him is exaggerated in the memoirs of a writer from the middle of the second century as preserved in a church history written in the fourth century:

[James] was holy from his birth; he drank no wine or intoxicating liquor and ate no meat; no razor came near his head; he did not smear himself with oil, and did not go to the baths. This one alone was permitted to enter the Temple sanctuary, for he did not wear wool but linen. And alone he would enter the Temple and be found on his knees, praying for forgiveness for the people, so that his knees grew hard like a camel's (Eusebius, *Church History* 2.23.4).

The same source also tells of the death of James in A.D. 62.

Yet, the address of the Letter of James shows that it was intended not for Palestinian Christians but for those who lived in the area that Paul had evangelized. Further, the quality of the Greek (which shows the facility that permits plays on words) and the rhetorical form of the writing indicate that the author had received a good pagan education. This is not to say, however, that the writer was a gentile. Although the literary form is that of a pagan moral tract, the morality it teaches rests firmly on Jewish tradition, so much so, in fact, that there are only two explicitly Christian references in it. Yet, some of the statements in it are very close to sayings attributed to Jesus in the Gospels. The likelihood, then, seems to be that the Letter of James was written for Hellenistic Jewish Christians in Asia Minor. An indication of date comes from 2:14-26 in which there is a refutation of an understanding of grace versus works that seems directed against a group who had misunderstood Paul. Although Paul was misunderstood often enough in his lifetime, this particular misunderstanding seems to represent something later, something toward the end of the first century.

Although it also comes from a Jewish Christian tradition, the Letter of Jude is much cruder than that of James. It is an attack upon members of the Christian community who are guilty of an error that is not spelled out in any detail. Instead, their morals are attacked, and all kinds of dire things are predicted for them on the basis of apocalyptic Jewish writings. This apocalyptic character may account for the location of Jude in the New Testament between the

Johannine epistles and the Revelation, a location that otherwise is difficult to understand, since it has Jude separate writings from the Johannine school while itself being removed from the other catholic epistles. Apocryphal Jewish writings are cited nowhere else in the New Testament. Jude's dealing with dissent by attacking the morals of the dissenters and predicting unpleasantness for them in the hereafter represents a rather low point in the effort of emerging catholicism to deal with the threat of heresy.

The Letters of James and Jude represent Jewish Christian traditions that still honored the names of the brothers of the Lord. Since the name of Peter was also associated with Jewish Christianity, it might be expected that I Peter would also come from such a community, but in fact its theology is much closer to that of Paul. Since the epistle gives as its dateline "Babylon," a code name for Rome, and since it was probably written near the time of I Clement, which speaks of the martyrdoms of Peter and Paul in that city, I Peter may come from a Paulinist group there. If so, it would furnish the irony that the earliest treatment of Peter as head of the church at Rome would come from a group of Christians loyal to the example of Paul.

Like James, I Peter is written in excellent Greek. It has two main themes: the newness of the life in Christ of its addressees and suffering. Through much of the document, this suffering is spoken of in very general terms, and much of the document has the form of a table of duties for members of a household. Thus it sounds as though it could have been written as a sermon for baptism. Indeed, some scholars have gone so far as to suggest that it was actually a liturgy for baptism, although it has very little liturgical flavor to it.

But beginning with 4:12, it begins to sound as though real persecution was imminent.

Beloved, do not be surprised at the fiery ordeal which comes upon you to prove you, as though something strange were happening to you. But rejoice in so far as you share Christ's sufferings, that you may also rejoice and be glad when his glory is revealed.

The way that the verses above and 5:10 pick up themes that are given in 1:6-7 shows that as we have it I Peter is a unified composition. Nevertheless some scholars think that it is a baptismal sermon that was rewritten as an exhortation to a Christian community in danger of persecution. A time around the end of the first century, when persecution was feared from the Emperor Domitian, seems as likely a date for this writing as can be established.

Whoever wrote I Peter, one can be fairly certain that the same person did not write II Peter. While it is true that the author of the second epistle is familiar with the first, it is also clear that he or she knew several other volumes in the New Testament. For instance, 2:1–3:3 is essentially the same as Jude 5–19, and most of the other verses of Jude have parallels somewhere in II Peter. Scholarly analysis has shown that Jude did not use II Peter and that the two do not depend on a common source; thus the author of II Peter copied from Jude. Furthermore, the author treats Paul's letters as Holy Scripture in 3:15-16 and is concerned with how the authority of Paul is invoked by a group of heretics who interpret Paul differently. Thus II Peter comes out strongly in favor of authoritative biblical interpretation in the spirit of emerging catholicism: "First of all you must understand this, that no prophecy of scripture is a matter of one's own interpretation, because no prophecy ever came by the impulse of man, but men moved by the Holy Spirit spoke from God" (1:20-21).

While using Jude, II Peter also changes it. Gone are the citations of apocryphal books found in Jude. Indeed, the thought world is very different from that of Jude's Jewish Christianity. Instead of its apocalypticism, here one confronts the vocabulary of pagan Greco-Roman piety. While it insists on the accuracy of early Christian expectations that Christ would return soon, it changes the meaning of the expectation entirely. To begin with, it is defended on the basis of Psalm 90:4, which says that for God a thousand years are but a day, thus emptying "soon" of any content. Further, this second coming is not discussed in the vocabulary of Jewish apocalyptic but in that of the doctrine of the conflagration of Stoic philosophy.

For all these reasons, II Peter is regarded as the last book of the New Testament to have been written, being dated somewhere between A.D. 125 and 150. This would put it near to the high tide of Gnostic threat to Christianity and would thus make its efforts to safeguard Paul from heretical interpretation very understandable. To give authority to its argument, it claims to be the last will and testament of Peter (1:13-15), thus using the literary form that is met in Genesis 49, John 14–17, and II Timothy. By the time it was written, the church had gone a long way toward becoming an institution in society, having settled down for the long haul of history.

THINGS TO THINK ABOUT

1. What is your reaction to learning about the variety of early Christian communities?
2. Do you agree or disagree with the statement that church life has to be institutional? Is that a good or bad thing?
3. Do you think that Christianity has benefited or suffered from acquiring a canon of scripture, creeds, official teachers, and sacraments?
4. Is there one clear pattern of ordained ministry in the New Testament?
5. How do you like the picture of non-Pauline Christianity given by the catholic (General) epistles?

Here We Have
No Abiding City

A Vision of the End

No book in the Bible has suffered such a variety of interpretation as the Revelation. (Note that it is only one: Revelation, not Revelations, as it is sometimes called.) It was one of the last books to be recognized as a part of the New Testament canon, not being universally included until after the fourth century. Indeed, the great German leader of the Protestant Reformation, Martin Luther, did not believe that it should be considered a part of Holy Scripture, and there are sensitive Christians today who feel the same way.

Yet, the Revelation is crucial to the understanding many Christians have of their religion. They see it as a timetable for the end of the world and try to locate the place of their own time in the countdown so that they can tell how much longer the world will exist and, therefore, be prepared when the end comes. Most of the great tyrants of history have been identified in their own time with 666, the beast of the Revelation.

During World War II, someone tried to convince Dr. Henry Sloane Coffin, president of Union Theological Seminary, that the German dictator was the beast, pointing out that the words *Adolph*, *Hitler*, and *Fuhrer* (Hitler's chosen title, meaning "leader") contain six letters each. Dr.

Coffin replied that Hitler spelled his first name *Adolf*, with only five letters, and that the *u* in the German word for leader has over it the two dots of an umlaut, a shorthand form of the letter *e*, which makes *Fuehrer* a seven-letter word. Thus Hitler was 567 rather than 666. Rather than convincing the man, however, this only illustrated to him Hitler's diabolical cleverness in thus being able to conceal his true identity.

Similar efforts have been made to identify the beast with Napoleon, Kaiser Wilhelm, Russian tsars, and Joseph Stalin. Much of the distinctive doctrine of the Jehovah's Witnesses grows out of their understanding of the Revelation. In recent decades, one of the biggest selling books has been Hal Lindsey's *The Late, Great Planet Earth*, an effort to prove that the world was going to end soon because Russia, China, and Israel were doing things predicted in this book and elsewhere in the Bible.

On the other hand, William Stringfellow has argued that the wealth and self-indulgence of modern-day America makes it more like the persecuting empire than the threatened church in the Apocalypse.* And the theme of Revelation has been picked up literarily in Blasco Ibanez's novel about World War I, *The Four Horsemen of the Apocalypse*, and a film about the war in Vietnam is called *Apocalypse Now*. These influences can get drawn out; Ibanez's novel was made into a film starring Rudolph Valentino that was popular enough to inspire someone to call a great Notre Dame backfield "The Four Horsemen of the Apocalypse."

This variety of interpretation even extends to New Testament scholars who are committed to using the

---

*A transliteration of the Greek word translated as "revelation." It has a root meaning of "uncovering" or "bringing out of hiding."

historical-critical method. Their general agreement about
method has not led them to any consensus about the
meaning of this book. Recent interpreters have thought that
the book is essentially a tract in liberation theology, calling
for an end to the economic exploitation of the poor or that
the John who wrote it was John the Baptist or that the book
is not really apocalyptic; instead it is "a critical discussion of
already existing apocalyptic views and speculations"
(Helmut Koester, *Introduction to the New Testament* [Philadel-
phia: Fortress Press, 1982], p. 248). Others get carried away
by all the numbers and begin to see wheels in wheels. Thus
some of the scholarly readings of Revelation seem about as
strange as the book itself, and one is tempted to say to their
authors what the Roman governor Festus said to Paul:
"Your great learning is turning you mad" (Acts 26:24).

Nevertheless there is a sort of mainstream of interpretation in which most scholars find themselves. It begins by
recognizing that the Revelation belongs to the type of
writing that is called "apocalyptic." The only other entire
book of this kind of literature found in the Bible is the book
of Daniel. Yet, this sort of writing has become very familiar
to scholars because of the many examples of it that occur in
the Dead Sea Scrolls and other intertestamental literature.
The characteristics of apocalyptic, not all of which are
shared by the Revelation, are several. Such a book is usually
pseudonymous, claiming to have been written by some
worthy of the past. It takes the form of a foretelling of the
future. Since it was written in the period that it was written
for, most of the book—the part that appears to predict what
has already happened—will be prophecy after the event.
Thus, since all of that part of the prophecy had already come
true, the reader will have good reason to expect that the real
prophecy in it—the predictions about what will happen
after the writing—will come true as well. And this writing is
usually so symbolic or even allegorical that it is often hard
for modern readers who have lost the key to know exactly
what it refers to.

The author of Revelation claims to be named John and further claims that the content of this book was dictated to him by an angel in an ecstatic vision (1:1-11). Thus, while other New Testament books give no indication that their authors thought of them as inspired writings, this one claims to be revelation. The author considered what he wrote to be prophecy in the sense that it foretold the future, "what is and what is to take place hereafter" (1:19). The book is written in a symbolic language that is chock-full of biblical allusions. Its Greek is that of a person more at home in one or more Semitic languages than in the tongue in which the book is written.

Christian imagination has sought to identify this John with others mentioned in the New Testament, especially the son of Zebedee, who was an apostle and who was also thought to have written the Fourth Gospel. Both the theology and the literary style of this author are so different from that of the author of the Johannine Gospel that most scholars find it hard to believe the same person wrote both. And, as noted above, it is unlikely that the beloved Disciple who lies behind the tradition of the Fourth Gospel was the son of Zebedee. Further, it seems unlikely that the author of Revelation could be the apostle either. The main reason for saying that is that this work appears to have been written more than sixty years after the ministry of Jesus during which an apostle would have already been an adult. It seems unlikely that a man at least in his eighties could have written this work.

Thus the writer was a Christian prophet named John who was probably a Hebrew- and/or Aramaic-speaking Jew born in Palestine who had migrated to the area in western Asia Minor evangelized by Paul and who went from church to church often enough to be very familiar with the seven congregations to which he wrote. At the time of writing, he was a Roman political prisoner on the island of Patmos, just off the Turkish coast to the southwest of the cities of the seven churches to which he wrote. Since chapter 17 makes it as clear as highly symbolic language can be that the enemy of the church was the Roman emperor and since the time of writing was a period in which the Roman emperor was worshiped as a god (19:20), the best guess is that the Revelation was written during the reign of Emperor Domitian in the closing years of the first century.

This is not to say, however, that Domitian actively persecuted the church or even that there was a marked crisis at the time the Apocalypse was written. Neither of those statements can be proved. The author claims that he was imprisoned, that another person had been killed, and that he expected 144,000 people (a highly symbolic number) to die before the troubles of the church were over. But they had not died yet! So what we have is not an account of a persecution, but a statement that persecution is expected. Notice that the author was trying to convince his addressees that they were in a crisis. If they had to be convinced, it could not have been the sort of obvious crisis that an active persecution would have been.

One of the sanest recent studies of the Revelation is *Crisis and Catharsis: The Power of the Apocalypse* by Adela Yarbro Collins, who has taught New Testament at McCormick Theological Seminary and now teaches it at Notre Dame. She has made use of sociological and anthropological studies of modern groups that expect the end of the world and points out that their beliefs do not seem to have been responses to particular social crises or intense economic deprivation. Rather they appear to be responses to what she calls "relative deprivation" in situations in which the expectations of groups are not consistent with their actual situations.

A case in point would be a South Sea island that had been "discovered" and occupied by Europeans or Americans. While the indigenous people may have been happy enough before the arrival of the Westerners, the sight of all the cargo unloaded on the docks for the foreigners could have evoked in the islanders a sense of relative deprivation that found expression in a "cargo cult" that expected a messiah who would make such trade goods available to them. There are numerous instances on record of such things having happened.

By analogy, Collins is able to say: "It was the tension between John's vision of the kingdom of God and his environment that moved him to write his Apocalypse" (p. 106). His expectations of the coming kingdom seemed very inconsistent with the social reality he faced as one imprisoned for his faithfulness in a society that was becoming increasingly hostile to Christians. Then Collins goes on to point out how the Revelation's imagery of letters to churches, seals, trumpets, bowls, and all the other things that can be counted in sevens served a very useful purpose for those to whom it was written. It gave them a faith standpoint from which they could look at their situation and thus have confidence to face it. They could bear the struggle ahead if they knew that it was important in the eyes of a God who could and would overcome the powers of evil that beset them.

Some Christians today wonder why the church should keep such a book in its canon. It seems to be a prediction of the end of the world along with the fall of the Roman Empire, a prediction that obviously did not come true at the expected time. Also, it seems to take a great deal of glee in violence to the enemies of the church—an understandable, but not very Christlike, attitude. What should modern Christians make of this book? Collins points out that the Revelation has been a strong word of hope to many people down through the centuries whose strength had seemed almost gone. And, although there are differences, she sees Revelation assisting in the two functions of the church as what Johannes Metz has called an "institution of socially critical freedom." One of these functions is to recognize and resist as idolatrous the tendency of any nation or institution to regard itself as perfect the way the Roman Empire did in the time of John. The other is to call the church to get behind any movement that resists these tendencies by supporting efforts to achieve the fuller promises of the kingdom of God, which include freedom, peace, justice, and reconciliation.

A People En Route

Since the Revelation is both the last book of the Bible and the one that gives most attention to the end of the world, it could be thought to be the ideal one to consider last in a book about the New Testament. Another has been chosen, however, for reasons that one hopes are adequate and will become apparent. This book is almost as devoid of parallel in the New Testament as the Apocalypse is. It is called "The Letter of Paul to the Hebrews," but many scholars agree with Reginald Fuller that it is not a letter, it is not by Paul, and is not to the Hebrews. Although the Greek-speaking church in the East liked it from very early on because of its use of a familiar philosophical vocabulary, the Latin-speaking church of the West did not really accept it until well into the fourth century. Struggling with the reconciliation of Christians who had wavered during times of persecution, the Western church was troubled by the way that Hebrews says there is no forgiveness of sins committed after baptism (6:4-8).

The uniqueness of Hebrews involves the paradox that it is at once one of the most Greek and one of the most Jewish books in the canon. The author wrote even better Greek than Luke and, further, seems immersed enough in Greek thought to use concepts and vocabulary that derive ultimately from Plato. At the same time, the argument of the entire book consists of very technical interpretations of the Hebrew Scriptures, a kind of argument that could only have arisen in a community that accepted the Hebrew canon as its final authority and thus was given to the most minute analysis of its meaning.

While precisely the same sort of interpretation occurs nowhere else in the New Testament, it is very similar to at least two kinds of interpretation engaged in by Jewish groups at the time. One has been alluded to already, the allegorical interpretation that Hellenistic Jews in Alexandria, Egypt developed in imitation of the way Stoic philosophers interpreted the works of Homer. The most famous practitioner of this method was a very distinguished Jew named Philo. Being, on the one hand, deeply learned in both biblical study and pagan philosophy and, on the other, very worried about the assimilationist tendencies of young Jews like his nephew, he wrote to prove that the religion of the Hebrew Scriptures is both consistent with and superior to the best in pagan thought. He would thus use allegorical interpretation to show that, for example, names in Genesis or the legal provisions of Leviticus were veiled ways of talking about the truths that Greek philosophers taught. Indeed, he went so far as to suggest that all the best ideas of the philosophers had been borrowed from the Hebrew Scriptures.

The other sort of interpretation that Hebrews reminds us of was practiced by the community that wrote the Dead Sea Scrolls. It is seen most clearly in a scroll that seeks to explain the book of Habakkuk as a veiled prophecy of the rise of their community. Scholars sometimes distinguish between allegorical interpretation and what they call typological interpretation. Allegorical interpretation treats a document as having been written in a code by which each thing stands for something else. Thus Augustine was able to preach on the miraculous catch of fish by saying that the sea was the world, the fish were souls, the net was the preaching of the gospel, and the boat was the church. Typological interpretation, on the other hand, sees a common principle operating between situations in the Hebrew Scriptures and those of the new covenant. Thus the exodus would be a type of the redemption brought by Christ, a promise, in effect, that he was to fulfill. Or the manna on the Exodus could be thought of as a type of the eucharist.

In terms of this distinction, Hebrews discusses many of the same religious institutions of the former covenant that Philo interprets in an allegorical way, but the interpretation in Hebrews is typological. The institutions of the Torah are considered to be promises that Christ fulfilled. In addition, there is a Platonic element in Hebrews. In the thought of Plato, what is really real is not all of the material objects that one encounters while existing in time. No, each of those objects is a mere shadow of the eternal idea of that category of objects. Thus all chairs, for instance, could be thought of as sharing chairness, that which makes a chair a chair and not something else. Yet, each individual chair would be only imperfectly a chair because it has qualities that distinguish it from other chairs, qualities then that are a departure from chairness. Perfect chairness—the ultimate reality of chairs—is possessed only by the eternal idea of the chair, an ideal that is purely spiritual. This ideal chair is the pure form of the chair, the form that informs the matter of all concrete material chairs without itself being any of them.

This Platonic strain in the thought of Hebrews may be seen in 8:5, where the author is interpreting Exodus 25:40, a verse from the story of how Moses was to construct the tent that was to serve as the Temple while the Israelites were going home from Egypt. That verse refers to a model of all the furnishings for the tent that was shown to Moses on Mt. Sinai. By the interpretation in Hebrews, that model was the "real" Temple, the Platonic idea of the Temple, an idea in which any concrete Temple on earth participated only incompletely. "[The priests in the tent] serve a *copy* and *shadow* of the heavenly sanctuary" (8:5; italics added).

This combination of Platonic and typological interpretation allows the author of Hebrews to argue that Christianity replaces the religious system of the Temple of Israel. Jesus is understood as the great high priest. His death was the perfect sacrifice because it had a perfect victim (Christ himself) who had to be offered only once. This sacrifice inaugurated a new covenant, a new set of conditions for the proper relation between God and the people of God. In this way, Christianity is treated as having succeeded and replaced Judaism. Thus the religion of Israel was the promise, the "type and shadow," of the new covenant established by Christ. Further, Jesus' death was the entry of the great high priest into the heavenly Temple, which is understood to be the real one that was shown to Moses on Sinai. Jesus' entry there makes it possible for human beings to go there; he is their "pioneer" or "trailblazer" in this regard. Thus the salvation brought by Jesus is real salvation, while that of Judaism is regarded as merely a shadowy representation, a promise of the better things to come.

Several other figures of speech are used to make the same argument in Hebrews. For instance, the early chapters are an argument that Jesus is superior to some of the religious figures most respected in Judaism: the angels, Moses, and Joshua. In talking about this, the author engages in an interpretation of Psalm 95, which ends with reference to the lack of faith of the Israelites on the exodus. Because of that, the twelve tribes were forced to wander in the wilderness for forty years before entering the land of promise so that the unfaithful generation could die out. Psalm 95 refers to this by having God say, "Therefore I swore in my anger that they should not enter into my rest" (Ps. 95:11). Thus entry into the land is referred to as "rest," and the author picks up the concept of "rest" to designate the salvation accomplished by an adequate religious system. So entering God's rest in Hebrews is the same thing as entering the heavenly sanctuary where Christ the great high priest is ever making intercession for his followers. Neither Moses nor Joshua made it possible for the people of God to enter that rest, but Jesus did.

Hebrews does not begin with the salutation and greetings that are characteristic of letters, and indeed only the last chapter or maybe the last four verses sound like the closing greetings of a letter. It does not say who it was from or who it was written to, although the reference in 13:23 to Timothy may be an effort to associate the document with a community connected with Paul; there are other Pauline aspects to the book, such as considering the death of Christ to be a sacrifice. The rest of the book, however, which alternates between biblical interpretation and exhortation, seems more like a sermon or group of sermons than a letter. There is so little specific internal evidence about the author and audience that scholars continue to argue over whether Hebrews is correspondence or preaching.

The main thing that can be said about the nature of the document is that the author seems worried about the flagging interest of his addressees and is writing to stimulate them to renewed enthusiasm and effort. Since his doing so is based so completely on technical interpretations of passages of the Hebrew Scriptures, he must be writing to a community who accepted them as authoritative. And since his main line of thought is the superiority of the Christian covenant to the Mosaic one that preceded it, he must be writing to people who originally belonged to the Mosaic covenant and who are now in danger of falling back into it. Thus his audience may be a group of Hellenistic Jewish Christians who were in danger of lapsing. Since I Clement, which was written in the 90s of the first century, makes allusion to Hebrews, this epistle would have to have been written earlier enough for it to have time to become known in Rome. That is about all that can be said about when, why, or by whom Hebrews came to be written. Already in the third century Origen said: "God only knows who wrote it."

Chapter 11 begins with a familiar definition of faith as "the assurance of things hoped for, the conviction of things not seen." It then goes on to give examples of this faith in the great heroes of the Hebrew scriptures as people who looked forward to the salvation Jesus would bring; this salvation was what they hoped for with assurance, the invisible thing they were convinced existed. Because of this unfulfilled faith, this longing and anticipation, they are described as "strangers and exiles on earth" (11:13). Thus it is said of Abraham:

By faith he sojourned in the land of promise, as in a foreign land, living in tents with Isaac and Jacob, heirs with him of the same promise. For he looked forward to a city which has foundations, whose builder and maker is God. (11:9-10)

Thus the children of Israel were a people on a pilgrimage, a people in transit, a people *en route*.

Yet, very similar language is used about Christians in the last chapter: "Here we have no lasting city, but we seek the city which is to come" (13:14). Even though the faith anticipated by the patriarchs and matriarchs has come to pass in Christ, his followers will not have it in full possession until they enter into the heavenly sanctuary into which he, as their great high priest and pioneer, has already gone. Meanwhile they, too, are "strangers and pilgrims" (11:13 KJV). Yet they can already enjoy that salvation as an assured hope; they can have the conviction that what they do not yet see already exists. They can do so because in their pilgrimage they can meditate as did the author of Hebrews on the Holy Writ that has been written for them. This is as true of Christians today as it was of the audience for whom Hebrews was originally written.

THINGS TO THINK ABOUT

1. Do you think Revelation should be included in the canon? Why?
2. Does it surprise you that even scholars cannot agree about the meaning of Revelation?
3. What valid insight do you get from Revelation?
4. Do you find the interpretation of scripture in Hebrews hard to follow? Do you see ways in which a similar kind of scripture reading would be helpful in your own spiritual life? Explain.